Sustainable Smallholding

Lorraine Turnbull

Copyright

Copyright 2020 Lorraine Turnbull

Publisher: Fat Sheep Press

British Library Cataloguing in Publication Data

A CIP catalogue for this book is available from The British Library

ISBN 978-1-9163890-5-2

This is a new, revised and expanded version of the book previously published as The Sustainable Smallholders' Handbook (2019)

The Author's sincere thanks go to all who contributed to this book.

About the author

Lorraine Turnbull wanted to be a farmer since she was five years old. After running a successful gardening business in Glasgow she uprooted herself and her family and moved to a run-down bungalow with an acre of land and an Agricultural Occupancy Condition in Cornwall. She retrained as a Further Education teacher and taught horticulture at both adult & further education level, whilst running a one-acre smallholding. After working as a Skills Co-ordinator for The Rural Business School, she began commercial cider making in 2010.

In 2014 she was recognised for her contribution to sustainable living by winning the Cornwall Sustainability Awards Best Individual category. She successfully removed the Agricultural Occupancy Condition from her home before moving to France. Her first book, *The Sustainable Smallholders' Handbook,* was published in May 2019.

Lorraine now lives in the Dordogne with her husband, cocker spaniels and sheep. She continues to write on a smallholding or land-based theme.

Connect with Lorraine:

http://www.facebook.com/SustainableSmallholding/

http://www.twitter.com/LorraineAuthor

http://www.instagram.com/lorraineauthor

Contents

INTRODUCTION

This book is a new, revised, and expanded version of the book previously published as *The Sustainable Smallholders' Handbook* **(2019).**

This new guide to sustainable smallholding can help you take the smallest of steps towards self-sufficiency, and you can even start today! Whether you have a smallholding or a small urban home, this book will help everyone on their journey towards sustainability.

As an ex-agricultural college tutor, Skills Co-ordinator for the Rural Business School in Cornwall, winner of Best Individual in the Cornwall Sustainability Awards 2014, and smallholder of many years' duration, I feel that it is important to encourage aspiring, new and struggling smallholders, rural businesses and individuals to make the best of the assets and skills they have. The decision to write this new and expanded version of a well-received first book was taken in response to readers' demands for more information on certain subjects, and to ensure that information is up to date, relevant and topical.

This book will help you to identify little things that you can "tweak" that will help you live more sustainably, and save you money too. There are many suggestions for diversification, for sustainable practice and other ways to make your "little piece of heaven" more profitable and productive, wherever

11

you live. Although the book is primarily aimed for those living in the UK, it may prompt international readers to look at their own practices and adopt some money-saving, money-making and sustainable projects.

I am lucky to have many eco-friendly and smallholder friends, and it greatly encourages me to see an increasing awareness and yearning to live sustainably. Some of these friends have kindly contributed case studies for this book, and you can learn how various people, all over the UK, live from their land. In 2020 the Covid-19 pandemic finally made people sit up and take notice of food supply and food security, and whilst the disease and its effects have decimated some businesses, the ability to produce food and supply it on a local basis has increased the status and worth of UK smallholders, farmers and gardeners. With a temperate climate and a varied natural geography, the UK has an opportunity to develop its world-class agricultural dominance, and producers of all sizes to supply many of the needs of its consumers.

As a land-based tutor, the favourite question I was asked at the end of most of the smallholding and cider courses that I organised was "How on earth can you make enough money?" Whilst this book is entitled, *Sustainable Smallholding,* it's about so much more than just smallholding. It's about making your sustainable life a success, whether this is in monetary or satisfaction terms. Health, contentment, job satisfaction and living a country life are treasures in themselves, and this book aims to get the reader to think more holistically about "Living the Dream".

There is a vast amount of diversification ideas and projects within this book simply because every smallholder or rural business is different, with different geographical locations and constraints, different skill sets and varying amounts of land, assets and cash to invest in their project. This isn't a recipe book to follow to the letter; rather, I would encourage you to "think outside the box", cherry-pick preferably more than one idea or project, spread the risk, make the most of working to suit your personal needs and hopefully enjoy a sustainable and self-funding (even profitable) "Good Life".

Lorraine Turnbull

December 2020.

Chapter 1
Miniscule to Mighty

The UK produces food from an array of agricultural and horticultural businesses and private land. Some are vast factory farms, some are smallholdings of a few acres and some are based in gardens and plots of land all over the UK. One size does not always fit all, thank goodness. Whilst larger farms concentrate on cultivating vast tracts of land for arable crops or huge numbers of livestock, these producers tend to sell their produce to specialist buyers. This book is not aimed at helping them, although many of the ideas contained in the book are relevant to them also. It's aimed at the woodland owner, the smallholder and the garden owner who wants to make their business or hobby pay, or to be able to produce food for the family in the most cost-effective, sustainable way. I hope it will also help aspiring and struggling smallholders, or those considering off-grid living or buying land with the dream of some day building a rural home.

Bear in mind also that working on the land is a fluid and ever-changing creature. People age, and some develop conditions that necessitate changing working practices. I began smallholding at the relatively late age of 43. I was able to do most jobs on the smallholding that were required, and benefited from having a fit and healthy husband with whom I could split the load, especially at the start and the end of our time smallholding in Cornwall. After 10 years I was feeling the physical burden much more. I could still manage most of the jobs, but gave up contract lambing as it had become too physically demanding, and I began to rely more and more on volunteer and paid help during harvest time in the orchard and for cider production. Now, I live in France on a larger but less demanding smallholding. I have to face the onset of old age and everything that accompanies it, together with the possibility that one of us will possibly "pop our clogs" and leave the other to manage the fruit, vegetable garden, woodlands and sheep alone. The march of time does not put me off, and I will continue to live a sustainable and productive life. However, I continually examine how to make it easier.

If you want to live the "Good Life", please don't be put off. About two thirds of the smallholders and rural business owners I know are over 50 years old. Sadly, the cost of buying a smallholding or land on which to build a smallholding is beyond many youngsters starting out, and it's only when we have reached our middle years that we are able to finance such a dream. I wanted to be a smallholder since I was five years old, but had to wait decades before I was able to buy a suitable property, even if it was a run-down bungalow in a field with an Agricultural Occupancy Condition on it. You *can* do it, if you want it badly enough. If you are interested in reading my book, *Living on the Land: My Cornish Smallholding Dream*, it's widely available to buy, and is a warts-and-all true story of the ups and downs of our smallholding story.

There is no official definition of a smallholding, but it is generally accepted to be an agricultural property of up to 50 acres, but this generalisation covers a variety of properties, owners, and a multitude of uses. In the UK, there are crofts, small ex-farm-labourer cottages with parcels of land, and many houses subject to that little known and even less understood British institution, The Agricultural Occupancy Restriction. Smallholding can also be undertaken from country cottages, rectories, and village houses with attached or separate plots of land. Caravan dwellers, yurt dwellers and those living in communes or woodlands also number amongst those trying to make a sustainable living from the land. So, a smallholding isn't really a type of dwelling; it's a way of life.

Whether you have half an acre or fifty acres, you can make a profit or a loss on land. The saying "it's not the size that matters, it's what you do with it" is very true, especially in connection with agriculture, horticulture or forestry, and there is a vast difference between *surviving* and *thriving* on the land. Producing a steady, regular income from land at this time is not a walk in the park. I would argue that ALL agricultural activity is demanding, and set-up or conversion to organic production, for example, obviously has considerable additional costs, but organic produce can be profitable, especially if you are a producer with smaller acreage and multiple products to spread the risk. There is more about organic farming later in this chapter.

As far back as 1999, the US Institute for Food and Development policy brief indicated that farms less than 27 acres produced significantly higher returns than larger agricultural businesses. This is mainly due to specialisation in higher value produce (Policy Briefing no 4, p7). Many smallholders in the UK have far less land than this and run successful rural businesses. Clearly, quality matters more than quantity. There is no ideal plot size of land. A few books on self-sufficiency and smallholding will suggest a blueprint for an acre, or five acres or even ten acres, but remember business success isn't tied to land size. Each individual plot of land will be suitable for some uses and not others, and those living on it will be successful or not according to their skills, business acumen and motivation.

Now that the UK has left the European Union, there is a heated debate on whether subsidies will form part of the UK farming future. On one side, large landowners desire a similar subsidised scheme, but this will exclude smaller landowners including smallholders, who argue this will result in unfair advantage for larger producers.

As a result of both Brexit and the Covid-19 pandemic, experts and the public are finally accepting that there is a demand in the UK for a more sustainable, local system of food production and a desire for food security. Consumers are searching for quality local produce and are keen to support small producers. The producers in turn can add value to food, promoting animal welfare, traceability and rare breed support. Spreading the risk of financial failure by incorporating more than one income source on a smallholding or small farm increases the chance of success. For example, in my orchard in Cornwall, I produced apples, which in turn were processed to add value and I produced cider. The orchard was also home to some colonies of honeybees, which needed a small amount of space, but the value of the honey and wax was a valuable second stream of income. I also kept a flock of chickens for egg production in the orchard, and so the same piece of land supported three different income streams, and reduced the risk of financial failure.

For an interesting article on future farms read this article by Phil Moore, a reasonably new entrant to farming and a member of the Ecological Land Cooperative
http://sustainablefoodtrust.org/articles/funding-future-farms/

Spreading your risk will maximise your chances of success, and by having more than one product or service you can cushion against failure. In contrast, if you produce one product, or have agreed to supply one customer (for example, carrots to a supermarket), then beware that your risk is in that single crop being successful, and ensuring that your buyer is tied into an iron-clad contract, after you have invested serious capital in picking machinery or processing plant. Spreading the risk by having multiple products and/or multiple customers will make your business more resilient, especially if you have planned to spread income into the leaner months too. My main income streams at my smallholding were long-term furnished accommodation rental, cider sales and garden machinery servicing. But I also taught frequent one-day workshops, sold hatching eggs on an internet auction site, apple trees, rootstocks and scions.

If you intend to run a business from your smallholding – any kind of business – remember that you will be self-employed. This means that the buck stops with you. No one will pay you sick-pay or holiday money, and the bills will continue to drop on the doormat. For complete beginners or those contemplating buying a smallholding this can be very daunting. When we first moved to our one-acre in Cornwall, the amount of land was "huge" to us. What could we *do* with all that land? Within a year we were desperate to buy the two-acre field adjacent to us. A number of factors made us reconsider, and instead, we had an informal business meeting at the pub to decide our future direction. The outcome was that we decided to make the best possible use of the existing land, to maximise our profit and to look at niche products and services that no-one else provided locally. In marketing terms, we decided to develop our USP (Unique Selling Point).

Even on 1.2 acres we were both able to work part-time, support two children, and at the start, run two vehicles, whilst building our separate businesses on the smallholding. We worked hard, ate like kings, and our kids benefited

19

from growing up in the countryside. Most of all, we lived a lifestyle we have thoroughly enjoyed. Additional land may have been useful to us, if we had been younger, we argued, and we knew other smallholding couples *way older* than us who managed 21 acres and big animals. For us, we wanted to maintain control of what we wanted to do, not become overwhelmed or pressurised from a quickly expanding business that became no fun at all. We are all individuals, and for us, the lifestyle choice was the important factor.

Ask the Family

I'm now going to ask you a question that may shake your desire to live the smallholding life. It has to be asked sometime, and I think the earlier the better to avoid tears and tantrums. As you have chosen to read this book, I understand you have an interest, perhaps desperation to "live the dream". Is this incredible dream yours alone, or will you be starting out to fulfil your dream accompanied by a spouse/partner/children or parents?

Before you start trawling the internet for smallholdings for sale, let's just pop the kettle on and have a wee chat, just between us. There are some difficult subjects you'll need to consider and then discuss in detail with the others who'll accompany you on your dream journey. The minute you decide to up sticks, move to the country and start yogurt knitting for a living, tiny cracks may appear in your family unit. I'll put my hands up and admit straight away that my husband was more than happy with the idea. He came from a farming family, was a blacksmith by trade, as was his father, and loved country life. The older of my two children was horrified. She'd be leaving her friends, a busy social life and moving to Bumpkin Central! The world was going to end and it would be all my fault. The younger one was delightedly fantasising about quad bikes and killing things with axes, and my mother was distraught that her daughter was going to become…an agricultural labourer!

Fifteen years on and both children have now left University and will never work in agriculture, although both are very aware of the environment, and where their food comes from. They remember the good times as well as the uncertainty and hard work that was our smallholding life, and they certainly don't have any illusions that the world owes them a living.

Ask yourself, what is your motivation and is it shared by the family? Is the smallholding life something you have always wanted to do? Do you come from a farming background or have farming friends? Are you physically fit and able? Have you any experience with livestock and in the event, could you personally humanely kill an animal? If you are considering a simpler, cheaper way of life because you are struggling in the situation you are in at the moment how will you change this for the better? And finally, do you have an escape plan?

Working at any level in agriculture or horticulture is not utopia. This is a huge decision for everyone, and your life will be much easier if you can sit down with everyone and have a rational discussion about living the dream. Having all the facts and figures about how you intend to finance the dream will help get everyone on your side. Imagine it like presenting a business plan. After all, you will need all the practical and emotional support you can get, so getting your family 100% on board is really important. On the other hand, if you have a partner who is happiest in front of the television, or who screams every time a spider appears in the house, then perhaps you seriously need to think if this adventure is for them. Or, you could separate and find a more like-minded soul mate!

I cannot stress enough that one of the major reasons for failures in rural businesses is family/relationship problems.

If you have young children, you will have to stop and start chores repeatedly, work around them, and unless you have extended family nearby, invest in childcare. You will probably have to organise school runs and play-dates, although your children, if you train them to be sensible, will happily amuse themselves running through meadows, getting thoroughly filthy and playing with animals. Then they turn into teenagers and you really have your work cut out. Complicated teenage emotions and hormones take over, you will find you have become a taxi service, and may find it difficult to keep track of where your children are, who they're with and what they are doing, because you will be busy lambing, or fencing, or unblocking the overflow from the septic tank. The importance of education ends all those carefree years running wild, and the demands of getting grades and preparing for further or higher education become flashpoints, and could be the catalyst for change in the family dynamics. Although our children helped when asked, it was a very different story when they became teenagers, and as adults, it became clear they would never choose our lifestyle. Finally, children will drain your financial resources like a running tap.

Smallholding life is 24/7. All smallholders will tell you the days are long, especially in summer, and that you still have to care for animals and work in rain, hail and snow. Holidays are rare and short. At the end of our eighth year we finally managed to get five days away, and it was planned like a military exercise. Weekends to do activities with the children were difficult, which meant we were unpopular as well as tired. Christmas Day was a normal working day, and our social life revolved round farmers markets and auctions. Your calendar is governed by the weather and the timing of seasonal necessities, such as lambing, harvest and fencing. Agriculture is an endless cycle punctuated by a few golden moments and more than a few disasters. Cutting away the cover from our polytunnel at 3am in a ferocious October gale to save the metal structure has to be one of the highlights of 2009.

The local community may rally round with help and support at busy times to get the hay in or bring in the apple harvest, etc, and we have enjoyed sun-filled days watching the ducks mess about in their pond, evenings outside in sleeping bags watching meteors and the Milky Way, and spent many an indulgent hour in the orchard, watching and listening to the bees rumbling away in a cloud of pink and white petals. We have no regrets and wonderful memories.

If you think that living and working together in a demanding rural or land based business will 'pull you both together' then think again. If there are any cracks in your relationship to start with, then the monotony, long hours and isolation that can be rural life will magnify those cracks. You'll need a steady and strong relationship to start with when setting up any new venture, and both parties have to get something out of the deal; otherwise, there is no incentive to stay. Dreaming is all well and good, but it doesn't get the job done and will soon sicken your partner if you do all the dreaming and they do all the work.

A relationship where you can sit down and listen to each other is a partnership that will survive anything. If some project isn't working then you must say so, and decide how to move on. We carried on a small plant nursery business for three years trying to make it profitable, with John working off the holding to bring in money. Many factors contributed to the failure – poor weather for two summers, recession and the fact that local residents purchased plants at chain DIY stores. Facing reality and moving on from this was not the end of a dream, but a step in the right direction. It was better to stop doing something that was failing, and try something new. That's why this book is about looking at lots of options,

23

some of which will work for you, and some which won't.

If your family have no experience of country life, I would suggest attending an Open Farm Sunday event (**www. farmsunday.org**) and gauging the reaction. These annual events take place at the start of June, on a variety of farms all over the UK. Try a holiday on a working farm. Farm Stay UK offers B&B, self catering, camping & glamping breaks at different types of farms all over the UK (**www.farmstay. co.uk**). You can try your hand at lambing, milking, feeding the pigs, etc and experience a little of what real farming can be like, and it's a great opportunity to talk to farmers.

If you don't have children or they have left the nest, then consider volunteering at different times of the year on different farms or smallholdings. You'll get a balanced experience of the highs and lows of different seasons, of different skills required and of different enterprises. A week helping out during lambing time in The Dales sounds idyllic, but your third twelve-hour shift dealing with difficult births (and deaths), tired and irritable farmers, cold nights, aches and pains and the solitude may be enough for you to decide that certainly keeping sheep or any animals just isn't for you!

Financial Planning

How you are going to finance this dream? Properties are discussed in detail in the next chapter, but in addition to buying or renting a suitable property, you must have funds to live. A new business doesn't start to make profit overnight, and you'll need capital investment or other employment whilst you start the ball rolling. You'll need to budget for general living expenses, but also for training needs, insurances, building alterations if necessary, stock etc. Ensuring you have a substantial emergency fund is practically a necessity. Many people think that selling their house in the city or inheriting an existing house in the country will give them financial freedom to pursue a "return to the land". This is great, but you will also have to plan for on-going future costs. You will still need transport, animal feed and possible vet bills. Clothes and shoes will need to be replaced, and even if you plan to live out of a caravan or van, this needs to be paid for and a secure pitch found. Long-term living in a caravan or mobile home is not for everyone. It can be isolating, winters are hard and unromantic and the flip side to the freedom it gives is the difficulty of putting down roots and making long terms plans. Keeping a bricks and mortar address will allow you the safety net to access benefits and help if you need it, and having a long term plan with an escape clause is a good idea.

If you are starting any new project, whether it is a living in a van, or buying land or a smallholding to start a new life, you need a plan, and preferably a "Plan B" as well. Having a guaranteed income whilst you get started is a great idea, and can be dropped as your business grows and flourishes. There is no shame in considering a part-time supplementary income for one or both of you whilst you get your feet under the table. Knowing your strengths is key at this time. I was able to secure a well-paid, interesting part-time job at a local agricultural college, which was fantastic for us. I had access to a wealth of knowledge and could choose to update my training. This allowed John to start his machinery servicing business at home, which meant one of us could be on the smallholding all the time.

Of course, you will have to have a discussion of how you're going to divide the workload on your little piece of heaven. Working alone all day in all weathers doing hard, dirty jobs can be very demoralising and lonely. I can remember when the kids were at primary school, I had been chopping logs all day and lost track of the time. I hurried to the school to collect them with dirty working clothes and twigs and spiders in my hair, and can still remember the stares from some of the "yummy mummy" brigade, who obviously thought the school run was a fashion opportunity, and my embarrassed children, rolling their eyes, asking why couldn't I just be a "normal" mum.

Luckily for us, Cornwall was one of the poorest counties in England, and at that time benefited greatly from European Union funding for training and to help agricultural businesses to diversify and become more profitable. Training was greatly subsidised, and we took advantage to update our skills and to become occasional tutors. Although the UK has now left the European Union, there is still some domestic funding out there, both for training and capital investment, so you need to ask around to identify if any fit your circumstances and location.

Contacting your local agricultural College, Rural Development Programme, and Rural Grants and Payments Scheme
www.gov.uk/topic/farming-food-grants-payments/rural-grants-payments
is a good place to start to explore grant funding. Surfing the net may reveal more opportunities as this really does change constantly, and you need to read the small print to see if you qualify. Meantime, start drawing up a detailed business plan; you will need it for most funding and it's a good exercise to do to see exactly how the figures stack up. If you DO find some funding and want to apply, give yourself plenty of time, and ideally find someone who has successfully applied before to help you complete the application. There is usually a "right" way and a wrong way to complete the application.

If you have set a budget to fund the purchase of a suitable property, then you will also need to consider availability and location. Land and housing is much cheaper in the North of

26

the UK. Land with road access is perfect for a pony paddock, and will be sold by word of mouth before "outsiders" even know about it. Cheaper land may be exposed to the wind, be excessively steep, or have poor drainage, so doing some soil testing may be beneficial and influence what you can use the land for; it's not always the "bargain" it first appears. You may have to concentrate your search geographically to access the land you require, or to be near elderly parents, close to the city for work or schools. If this is the case be prepared to increase your budget, buy a run-down property or buy land with hope-value and live off-site.

There has been a surge of interest in living off-grid, whether as a couple, an individual or within a community, such as that at Tinker's Bubble in Somerset. Off-grid living is becoming increasingly popular in certain parts of the USA and Canada, and more common in the UK and Ireland. The variety of off-grid set-ups is huge, but gaining permission to live in the countryside is difficult in the UK and especially stressful if you have or intend to have a family. If this is a serious consideration, please research thoroughly, and look at the planning regulations in the next chapter.

Top Tips For Success

- DO get everyone on board at the start
- DO consider a supplementary income
- DO make a business plan
- DON'T underestimate the changes you face
- DO get some experience before committing
- BE realistic

Tax set-up and VAT

As part of your early planning, you need to take some

27

detailed financial advice from a good farm accountant. Explain your basic plan, your financial situation and your family composition, and ask what is the best way to register for tax liability. Most smallholders and rural businesses are self employed, but some are set up as Sole Traders, some as Limited Companies, some as Limited Liability Partnerships. You can find government information on self-employment by visiting **www.gov.uk/topic/business-tax/self-employed**

Depending on your business idea, you may be exempt from paying business rates if your land is used for agricultural, horticultural or forestry enterprises. This is a complex area; you must ensure you fully understand any liabilities you may incur, so be candid with your accountant.

If you are setting up a smallholding from scratch, do consider registering for VAT. Although it complicates accounting procedures, it may be extremely useful in claiming back VAT spent on capital investment, machinery, buildings etc. Again, your accountant is your friend. Ask him for a short list of items you can reclaim VAT on. Even if your intended business idea is to produce food (currently zero-rated for VAT), you can claim back much of the VAT spent on food processing machinery, packaging, tools, protective clothing and labelling, etc. If you have a tax office near you, phone them and ask to see an adviser if possible. It's my biggest regret, not registering for VAT when we first set up our own smallholding. Although I find book-keeping and accounting boring, there are now many simple software systems and packages to easily take care of this for you, and saving money, let's be frank – is never boring.

Finally, claim any and every grant or subsidy you are entitled to. This unfortunately gets harder to do every year, but as a reaction to leaving the European Union and the COVID-19 pandemic, the UK government is trying to kick start the economy again, and farmers, even small ones, matter.

Ask smallholding friends, ask questions on farming and smallholding Facebook pages and glean as much information as you can as to what is out there and if you are eligible to apply.

Time Management

Effective management of the time you spend on your smallholding or rural business is just as crucial as effective money management. Start to think of your time as a precious thing. There are only so many hours in a day and days in a week, but how you use this finite resource will determine your profitability and your ability to have a healthy work/life balance. After all, much of the attraction of smallholding life is to enjoy those fleeting yet important moments of watching the lambs gambolling in the paddock, the mating flights of the butterflies or just to sit enjoying a pint of your own cider with a mate in the orchard, discussing the performance of the local football team. If you are part of a couple or family unit then spending time with your "significant others" will go a long way to establishing household harmony and peace.

Establishing a successful working project takes a lot of planning, time and effort. There may appear to be endless hours of paperwork, sifting through the regulations and demands made upon livestock owners, and those running land based businesses. Poor weather can mean you must be able to switch tasks to keep working despite the elements, for example if you had planned a day of fencing, but it is too wet or windy to safely continue with this, then stop and move indoors to do book-keeping, send out invoices or clear that grotty shed you've been putting off for the last month.

Recognising that your time and labour are valuable commodities will also help you price your goods and services at a realistic level. My hourly rate for labour and routine jobs around the smallholding was a modest £15 per hour, but if I was teaching or giving educational talks my rate leapt to £22 per hour. I valued my knowledge and charged accordingly. The result was two-fold; firstly, I was enjoying a higher return for my time, and secondly, my well-being was improved, as I recognised that my skills were sought-after and in demand. As I earned more from my "specialisms", I could afford to reduce the time and labour spent doing menial jobs and concentrate on the more profitable ones. In turn, this enabled me to concentrate on cider production and teaching, whilst many of the simpler but labour intensive jobs could be completed by volunteers or contractors.

Careful planning, concentrating on high-value products in niche markets and building a good reputation will ensure business success. Work with the seasons and maximise natural resources to help you strengthen your life. Winter is a hard time for land-based businesses, but it's an ideal time for book-keeping, updating your marketing and social media, and building up those important family and social relationships that can get a little forgotten in the growing season.

A visual planning aid will help you plan your year. You could use a linear calendar year-planner or try a circular planner. For the circular planner, get a large piece of paper and draw a circle in it. Quarter the circle with straight lines and mark each quarter with an S for summer, A for autumn etc, almost like a compass. Then start to mark your main work periods onto the circle with a slightly smaller circle or part circle. You can release your inner creativity and use different colour pens for this (don't laugh – it helped me loads).

If your main business is, for example, garden machinery repair and maintenance, you should be busy from around March right through until October; so you would have an inner circular line (I used black) running from mid-spring through to the mid-autumn. From autumn through to early winter I drew a red line for my apple harvest, juicing & cider making. This left an ideal gap to do those fencing repairs, clearing out sheds or to fix leaking roofs. You may have some really small circular lines if you do short-term income sources – such as Christmas tree production or asparagus production, but mark all your income streams down and you will start to see when you are busy, or when you are quiet and could possibly introduce another income stream. The exercise will also show you the amount of time you spend on an activity. If the profit you realise is too small for the amount of effort you spend on it, then perhaps it's time to evaluate if it is worth continuing with it.

With a mixed smallholding you can have quite a few circular lines within the circle, and you can work seasonally and space activities fairly well. So, for my cider business, my circle started in September (with picking and pressing), and ran through December (when I finish pressing and have started to rack off the early fermentations). In February and March I began bottling, and sold the previous autumn's cider from Easter through till end of August. I managed to complete the paperwork and accounts in short gaps slotted in before the year began again. And this was just one strand of our business. It was time consuming, labour intensive but very profitable, and so was the mainstay of the smallholding side of the business.

All work and no play is no fun, so my "reward" was a fixed slot from mid February until the end of March when I went to my friend's farm in Launceston to help at lambing time. Whilst I went on my annual "busman's holiday" John taught one- and two-day blacksmithing and welding courses, and any spare time was spent fabricating small decorative items such as candle holders and door-knockers that could be sold at farmers markets, or on-line.

31

Organic Farming

Organic production is one of those subjects that tends to divide the agricultural community, but is a regular subject that is discussed when the subject of sustainable production comes up. Broadly speaking, the label "organic" generally reflects those farm production systems that work with nature, as opposed to conventional farming where pesticides, herbicides and increasingly hormones are used to conquer nature. There are farmers and food producers at both ends of the argument and many who are found in between. Some organic farmers refuse to use man-made chemicals of any kind – no pesticides, herbicides, no artificial fertilisers, limited use of animal vaccines or antibiotics, and focus instead on crop rotation, soil quality and biological diversity in order to combat issues that they encounter. You could argue that this is merely a return to traditional pre-industrial farming, which gained momentum in the post WW2 era. A combination of social unrest and energy shortages within the UK in the 1970s led to an increase in awareness of environmental factors and costs of food production. There was a nostalgic yearning for the "golden" age of farming and food production, whilst conventional farmers had to contend with negativity surrounding insecticides such as DDT, the incidence of vCJD (Mad Cow Disease) and Tuberculosis, and environmental degradation.

Naturally, consumer perception viewed organic production as healthier and more wholesome. In the UK, there are a number of organic certification schemes around, which you must register with before calling yourself an organic farmer or food producer. The largest is operated by the Soil Association (set up in 1946). All products claiming to be organic must display a certification number or symbol. There are mandatory inspections and it can take from 12 months to three years to get your status. You can access funding for converting to organic status through the Countryside Stewardship Scheme and via rural grants and payments. Some alternatives to the Soil Association include Organic Farmers & Growers, Organic Food Federation, and the Organic Trust Limited.

Of course, producers and consumers must educate themselves as to what words such as "organic" and those used on food labelling actually mean. There is a myth that organic food is produced with absolutely no pesticides, herbicides or fertilisers used, which is simply untrue. In fact, there is a list of chemicals, additives and animal treatments that organic producers can use. I have come across this lack of knowledge when talking to both producers and consumers of eggs. Producers often assume that as their hens have outdoor access this is enough to justify a "free range" status, which certainly isn't the case.

Conventional farmers and food producers counter the organic argument, stating that organic certification actually allows the use of some damaging chemicals including sulphur and rotenone (a naturally occurring herbicide, pesticide and piscicide); that food produced organically is no better than that produced by conventional means; and alleges that there is a human health risk when relying on fertilizer from animals in the food chain who are subject to neither anti-parasitic treatments or antibiotics. The argument will continue whilst there are gaps in the available knowledge, but the strongest argument against organic production is the cost involved. These usually include using more land for production, both for welfare reasons and to allow for resting of land, higher labour costs; and for smaller producers, the cost of registering and compliance to use the phrase "organic".

There are however, many areas where organic production is comparable with conventional production, and clever marketing can provide organic producers with a good income. Celebrity chefs and television shows have recently focussed on organic and sustainable food production methods, increasing consumer knowledge. Small producers can target this growing sector of the market by focussing their marketing and product packaging to highlight the "organic" status or "sustainable production" methods or even just the food miles used to bring "local" food to the consumer. Combining any or all of these labels is a win-win situation for the producer and the end consumer.

A quick look around supermarket shelves will reveal some assurance schemes, such as Red Tractor Scheme and Lion marked eggs, and many products extolling the virtues of their products with words like "Happy", "Natural", and "Wholesome"; which actually mean very little legally. Trading Standards have specific requirements for the correct wording and phrases on food packaging, but a glance at a comparable range of products will reveal a vast difference in packaging styles, and often only reading the small print on the rear will reveal more about the ingredients, origins and producer.

Naturally, the consumer wants the best product, but the challenge in these times of austerity is to persuade the consumer that buying the "best" product is preferable to buying the cheapest product. Often this means producing specialist luxury products or concentrating on out-of-season produce. Some niche organic products that are increasingly profitable are: baby food, dairy products and fresh local fruit and vegetables, especially via box schemes; organic pet food is another new niche product on the market. You really need to do your homework. I know of many small producers who aim to produce specific items for the Christmas market including Brussels sprouts, walnuts, paté, ducks, turkeys and liqueurs. By selling their produce via cooperatives such as Big Barn (**www.bigbarn.co.uk**) or Riverford (**www.**

34

riverford.co.uk), they can sell a substantial crop to a larger audience for a reasonable price.

I didn't apply for organic status for my cider production as I found the costs and length of time to await accreditation a pain. I never used any chemicals in the orchard at all, no fertiliser, no pesticides and no herbicides. I cut the grass and left the clippings on the surface to break down naturally. I pruned out and burned dead or cankered twigs and kept the orchard clean and tidy. As a result I enjoyed a thriving orchard with butterflies and moths, bats and barn owls. As the orchard matured, birds and animals deposited wild flower seed and my biodiversity increased, bringing more beneficial insects into play. If I had to choose a label to describe my farming practice, I think "traditional" sums it up best. As a sustainable, local producer I could sell a product that was honest and exclusive! Honesty about what I did and why, and sharing my working practices and ethos with customers, were key marketing practices. I didn't have to be organic certified – the consumer had the information they required to make an informed choice.

You will have to make the decision whether starting or converting to organic is the way forward for you. There are costs involved, but there is also some funding available out there to assist with this. Consumer demand is there and growing, but for a variety of reasons, organic farming and producers are decreasing in number. Reversion can be for many reasons, mainly a lack of success in the market; but many organic producers state that with the right marketing this should not be the case. An increased demand for local, seasonal food means that farmers are reconnecting with consumers at a local level, more jobs are created locally and the money goes around within that community. This leads to a corresponding increase in pride in local farmers, the local community and the countryside.

The UK has an opportunity to ensure that farming is sustainable. Defra have stated in their *Strategy for Sustainable Farming and Food* that farming has to date failed to perform economically, environmentally and socially and, until the recent exit from the European Union and Covid-19 pandemic, was a low-esteem industry. This is now changing, and the future for food production and farming in the UK is looking better. It's a good time for small, local producers to take advantage of the opportunities appearing in the UK market.

When things go wrong

We began our smallholding dream by starting a plant nursery. Half an acre was earmarked for hardy ornamental plant production, and my background in horticulture meant I was knowledgeable about propagation and market trends. Whilst we set up the infrastructure and began to cultivate plants, a recession engulfed the UK. Then the weather produced two very poor summers in succession. Sales were non existent. As a small producer I couldn't compete with cheap plant imports from Holland. Research revealed (too late) that every small independent plant nursery for miles around had failed. To tide us over John had to secure a temporary part-time job. Our savings disappeared. We were depressed and despondent, but we didn't just sit there waiting for our dream to disappear, and the bailiffs to arrive. We sat down and decided there was no point in throwing good money after bad, and looked at our existing skills, and how we could build a new business idea. I retrained as a teacher, and thereafter secured a part-time job at the local agricultural college. John used his engineering skills and nervously began self-employment as a garden machinery servicing and repair centre. The point is, we faced the situation and stopped doing the things that were losing us money, and replaced them with high-value services. Some friends already in the business coached me in commercial cider making, and encouraged me to sit and make a business plan to start my own. As the drain on our finances stopped and began to recover, I invested in some cider making equipment, and began small scale cider production. We had a rough couple of years, but by facing the situation and discussing it we managed to turn things around.

Sadly, farming can be very isolating, and problems can arise from all sorts of directions; the weather, poor prices, illness, family problems and debt are all known factors affecting people in land-based industries. The farming community understand all this because farming is a stressful occupation. If you feel overwhelmed, demoralised, lonely or ill please seek help. These things can creep up on you, but failing to listen to warning signs can lead to illness, injury and worse. Before you know it marital breakdown and the end of your dream are on the horizon. It's all right to take a break, or go visit friends if you feel it's all getting a bit much. Recognising stress is a good thing. Talking to someone can really help – you're not alone. The DPJ Foundation Charity supports members of the agricultural community all over Wales, **www.thedpjfoundation.co.uk**, The YANA Project helps farmers and those in rural areas, **www.yanahelp.org**, The Farming Community Network (**www.fcn.org.uk**) has a confidential helpline (+44 (0) 3000 111 999). They will all listen and will help you figure out the best way forward.

Balancing your time and energy is crucial; remember you are not living to work, you are working to live. And the best way to do this is to work smart. Here's a little recap on how to strive for success.

- Planning, Patience and Positivity all feature strongly in successful businesses. Make a realistic and detailed business plan.
- Start small and reinvest any profit into making the business grow.
- Paid employment is better than borrowing money.
- Apply for any and all relevant grant funding.
- Be flexible – businesses need to respond to trends and problems.
- Learn from your own and other people's mistakes. Talking is free!
- Add value to your produce.
- Spread the risk by having more than one string to your bow.

CASE STUDY – Blackaddon Allotments

Rich & Merryn Gillbard
Blackaddon Farm
Cornwall
www.blackaddonfarm.com
Facebook: Blackaddon Farm Allotments
Also on Twitter

Blackaddon Farm is a 220 acre traditional sheep and arable farm, which also offers a farm contract work service. Rich and Merryn started the allotment diversification in 2010 on 3 acres, providing 52 full & half-size plots to local people wishing extra room to grow their own fruit and vegetables. When all plots are rented out this provides an income of roughly £1000 per acre annually, which is 5-10% of the farm's total income.

With no previous allotment experience, the couple researched the possible diversification project for two years, and had invaluable help from The National Society of Allotment and Leisure Gardeners. They cite their first hurdle was dealing with the planning department, then dealing with the time to get the project up and running and into profit. There is also a new project, renting land to a vintage rally for a few days annually. The income this generates will be reinvested in the farm business.

With the onset of restrictions and fears of food security, the farm has continued to have a full register of allotmenteers, especially during Covid.

Quote – "Do lots of research and get lots of advice from the right people, compiling a file that you can show the relevant authorities. Pay attention to your paperwork, and keep a paper trail to refer back to. Keep slogging away at it and it will pay off. Would I do it again? – yes!"

Chapter 2
Properties, Planning & Permissions

For most of us the biggest purchase we will ever make in our lives is a property, and we require a mortgage to do so. This is the biggest stumbling block to a smallholder's dream, especially as mortgages are increasingly hard to secure, requiring a substantial deposit and steady income.

Some aspiring smallholders have financed their dream by selling a city property and some have inherited existing property or funds from a relative, but not all are this lucky.

Renting or farm tenancies are less desirable, but offer a way to enter the market and begin a land-based lifestyle.

Growing in popularity is the buying of land with "hope value", gambling on the opportunity to secure funding to gain permanent planning for a dwelling.

Renting & Agricultural Tenancies

Many private landowners use land agents or estate agents to manage and advertise agricultural properties; however, agricultural rentals and tenancies are not easily found and many change tenants without ever being advertised on the open market. If you manage to locate a property and it appears to fulfil your needs, please do take professional advice and scrutinise the terms and conditions specified on the lease and its tenure, as well as discovering if there are any restrictions on use. Remember, you may be risking your livelihood as well as your home. The agents, also, will wish to assure their clients that you are capable of regular rental payments, that your business use is legal, and may require references to prove your previous record of competency and responsibility, and that you will return the property back to them in at least the same condition, if not better.

The other main rental avenue to explore is that of local authority farm tenancies. These have been in existence since the 1890s, initiated to help young new entrants to agriculture, but due to government funding cuts, many councils have resorted to selling off tenant farms. The trickle of sales in the 1990s has swollen more recently, and as a result opportunities to secure a council farm tenancy are dwindling and competition is fierce.

Some private farm tenancies are still available from institutions such as the National Trust and National Trust for Scotland, the RSPB and the Duchy of Cornwall and large private estates. In many situations, the same family have farmed tenant farms for generations. You could also enquire at: Country Land and Business Association (**www.cla.org.uk**) and Scottish Land & Estates (**www.scottishlandandestates. co.uk**). If you are lucky enough to live in or can move to Scotland, please also have a look at the website of the Scottish Farm Land Trust. **www.scottishfarmlandtrust. org**, who are keen to purchase land and then rent this to new entrants and younger people who wish to farm small scale, ecological projects.

You can also have a look at the Ecological Land Coop, who support new entrant ecological farmers. The ELC model is to buy a parcel of land, divide it into smaller farm parcels, and apply for planning permission for AOC housing for each plot.

They also provide a shared infrastructure and support in the form of business planning and mentoring. Find out more here **https://ecologicalland.coop/about** .

Buying

Whilst renting is the cheaper option, you may rightly feel that it won't really give you the security to establish a long-term business. Buying is a much safer option if you can afford it, but gentrification is the problem. A house in the country, even if it is a run-down 1960s bungalow, is worth far more as a dwelling with amenity land than it would be as a smallholding with a dwelling. Most people dream of finding a ready-made smallholding, cottage with land or farm just ready to purchase. Of course, many people share this dream, so the price will be high and availability small. If you have the necessary finance for this option, then good luck in your search. Start looking at some of the elite rural estate agents.

The options available to purchasers include: buying a ready-made smallholding or farm, buying a rural or village dwelling without attached land, buying land with existing planning permission, and buying land with hope value – that is, purchasing land with no dwelling or planning for such. There are many things to consider, so we will look at each option in turn.

Crofting may be worth considering if you fancy a remote and challenging way of life in beautiful but remote areas of Northern Scotland and the Islands or indeed in Ireland. A croft is not just a small farm; it is a formal legal tenure of land, governed by the Crofting Commission Register of Crofts. There are more than 20,000 registered crofts in Scotland, of which around half are privately owned. Croft sizes vary, but most are around 12 acres (5 hectares), and consist in the main of rough pasture. There may also be an additional

43

"right to graze" on common land. This is not a lifestyle for the faint-hearted. A short growing season (60 growing-days annually less than the southern UK), limited local market and small, close-knit community life will deter all but the passionate and determined rural entrepreneur, willing to undertake "outside the box" opportunities to eke out a living. Crofting is very sympathetic to sustainable smallholding, but it must be recognised that profitability or self sufficiency will probably not be achieved. Having said this, demand is fierce, and advertising usually by word of mouth or very locally. The Scottish Crofting Federation maintains a list of crofts for their members. For more information visit: **www. crofting.scotland.gov.uk** and **www.crofting.org**

The popularity of the "country cottage" has priced it out of the reach of many. If you require a mortgage, and are looking at farms or properties with Agricultural Ties on them, your range of lenders will be slimmer still. Two sites worth looking at (and they offer a wealth of information) are: **www.ruralmortgages.co.uk** and **www.amconline.co.uk**. We secured a very small mortgage on our smallholding with a well known Building Society. They accepted the risk because the property was substantially priced, we were putting down a cash deposit of more than 90% of the value, there was no recession at the time, and we were existing mortgage customers with a perfect repayment record.

I will mention here that more and more aspiring and experienced smallholders and farmers are searching for properties abroad. Europe has recently seen a marked increase in the number of Britons who, Brexit aside, have simply decided that they have cheaper options, better weather and a better lifestyle outside the UK. For us, France offered a great lifestyle, the ability to tour the continent and land was incredibly cheap. We are now "in the system", have French healthcare, pay French taxes and will ultimately get French residency, but we are close enough to be able to visit family and friends as and when we need. If you are considering moving to France, consider buying my book, *How to Live the Good Life in France* (2020), which is widely available and full of advice.

A slightly less attractive option is to purchase a home with land unattached and live off-site from your future smallholding. This is certainly a cheaper option, but can be inconvenient when looking after livestock and for security purposes. We have friends who are successful smallholders with a 20 acre smallholding located about two miles from their village house. Whilst they have agricultural buildings on site and an office with toilet, kitchen facilities and a woodburner, it's not ideal. Security cameras, accessible from their mobile phone, allow them to remotely check both the property and livestock within buildings, but they would obviously prefer to live on-site and avoid having to travel backwards and forwards from house to holding. After ten years, they are now applying for planning permission for a small agricultural dwelling on site.

Buying land with existing detailed or outline planning permission can be expensive and again, not commonly found. Rural estate agencies are the best source for these, but you can also look online at the planning portal, **www. planningportal.co.uk** for areas you are particularly interested in.

Bare land is regularly marketed by land agents, rural estate agencies, and even by some local authorities. Purchasing land as a way to start a smallholding venture must be viewed cautiously. Assuming the land in question is agricultural land, you do not have an automatic right to erect buildings or a dwelling there. The UK countryside is heavily protected by strict planning laws, including the 1947 Town & Country Planning Act, designed to prevent swathes of housing appearing all over rural land.

Agricultural Occupancy Conditions

There is one way to buy an existing dwelling in the countryside that may fulfil your dreams and requirements, and is often temptingly priced, at say a third less than a similar open market property. This is the Agricultural Occupancy Condition, which is not the same as an agricultural tenancy which is described earlier in this chapter under "renting". An Ag Tie, Agricultural Tie, Agricultural dwelling, Agricultural Occupancy Condition and AOC are all the same thing.

Firstly, what is an Agricultural Occupancy Condition? Well, an Agricultural Occupancy Condition (AOC) effectively restricts the building of housing in the countryside. Prior to 2004, there was a very black and white difference between agricultural dwellings and ordinary residential housing; planning for residential use in the countryside was strictly opposed, unless it was to provide housing for agricultural, horticultural or forestry workers or to support the installation of travellers' sites. AOC properties restrict the occupant's use of the property and are also less attractive to conventional lenders when trying to secure a mortgage or loan on the property. The size of the purchasing market is severely reduced, when buyers realise they cannot comply with the terms of the AOC, and this restriction is reflected in the lower price. Unfortunately, this rather rigid distinction doesn't really take into account the more flexible and fluid employment world today, and a residency is either "agricultural" or not; which presents lots of problems with would-be occupants who work in the countryside but not technically in agriculture, forestry or horticulture.

You may come across AOC or "Ag Tie" properties advertised in rural estate agencies, or national newspapers. Attractively priced and, at first glance offering everything you need to begin a smallholding or rural business, they are a temptation to unwary prospective purchasers. Estate agents may or may not have detailed knowledge on AOCs, but discussing the wording of any AOC with a solicitor will soon reveal that buying such an encumbered property is not to be undertaken without ensuring you can fulfil the requirements. This section is deliberately long and detailed to explain what one is, how you can live with one, how you can apply for one, and how to get out of one.

Right now, I will explain a further complication. Firstly, UK planning basically changed for the separate countries within the UK with devolved parliaments, so there are different procedures and rules for England, Scotland and Wales. To further complicate things, there is a time division regarding AOCs, which prior to 2004 were pretty straightforward and applied all over the UK. Since devolution, and since August 2004, English planning law has developed, in that *new* AOC properties can benefit from a wider range of rural-based occupations. This is discussed below, after the traditional AOC restrictions. It also has to be stated that certain parts of the UK are more favourable towards sustainable development and establishment of smallholdings or rural businesses than others.

Firstly, a property built prior to August 2004 with an AOC attached to it restricts occupancy of the property to those working in or retired from agriculture, horticulture or forestry. There is a frequent general wording consisting of the phrase *"The occupation of the dwelling shall be limited to a person solely or mainly employed, or last employed, in the locality in agriculture, horticulture or forestry, or a widow or widower of such a person, and to any resident dependents."*

Many consist of the same wording, but some vary and you must examine the wording of any particular Condition to ascertain if you can fulfil the terms.

47

Some AOCs also include a Section 106 legal agreement tying the dwelling to the land. Local authorities are now adding this as a standard to new applications for permanent dwellings requiring AOCs. There is an argument that can be brought against having such a restrictive agreement imposed, as the presence of one means such an encumbered dwelling is unsuitable for securing a loan.

To further understand an AOC, let's look at the phrases within it.

Section 336 of the Town and Country Planning Act 1990 defines agriculture as: *horticulture, fruit growing, seed growing, dairy farming, the breeding and keeping of livestock (including any creature kept for the production of food, wool, skins or fur, or for the purpose of its use in the farming of the land), the use of land as grazing land, meadow land, osier land, market gardens and nursery grounds, and the use of land for woodlands where that use is ancillary to the farming of land for other agricultural purposes, and "agricultural" shall be construed accordingly.*

So to make this very legal definition a little easier to understand – to comply with the average AOC, the residents need to be actively farming. Keeping horses doesn't count unless those horses are used to work the land – i.e. for ploughing, or as forestry horses, or they are used to graze the land (and I think you would struggle to prove this last point). Keeping a few hens and sheep does NOT fulfil the AOC either. Bear in mind also, processing goods or offering services to goods not produced on your land technically counts as production or industry and not agricultural. So, if you have planted an orchard, but have to wait ten years for it to be productive and meanwhile you buy-in fruit to process into juice or cider, then this isn't adding value; it is not agriculture and it doesn't comply. Likewise, ancillary occupations, such as cheese making, tractor repairs, etc do not technically fulfil the definition of agriculture. The definition is vague and you will need to read up some court case studies to satisfy yourself, and possibly your solicitor, that you can indeed comply. One particularly helpful case is *Millington v Secretary of State for the Environment Transport and Regions v Shrewsbury and Atcham Borough Council June 1999.*

You don't need to read the court case itself, as I'll précis it here. Basically, Mr Millington started growing vines on his land, and started making wine from the grapes he grew. As the enterprise grew, some neighbours complained of the increase of traffic and other things and it ended up going to court. Anyway, the upshot of the case was that the judgement was on Mr Millington's side, and indicated that processing activities are ancillary to agriculture and part of the farming process when they are "reasonably necessary to make the product marketable or disposable to profit".

Naturally, interpretation is key, but for the uninitiated – it's the occupier's employment that is key in the wording of the AOC.

- "Solely or mainly" - your only or main
  occupation. Nowadays it's common for
  both occupants to work, whether full-time
  or part-time. The wording of the condition
  doesn't specify how many hours, nor the
  income required – so tread carefully here. If
  one person in the household is, say, a full-
  time farm worker (low wage) and the other a
  full-time doctor, then naturally there is going
  to be some doubt over the compliance of the
  wording of the AOC. However, if one member
  of the household is a self-employed, full-time
  forestry worker, and the other is a part-time
  shop worker, then this could be construed as
  fulfilling the terms of the condition.

49

- "Working" - Does any work need to be paid work? Recent case history has deemed it acceptable to be working in order to live self-sufficiently. Many part-time agricultural businesses also fail to make a profit. Whilst the tax man may question you over your ability to run a loss making business over a period of time, this does not necessarily mean you are in breach of the AOC (although, if you're endeavouring to prove you have a viable agricultural business in order to build a dwelling, this is a different matter).
- "Last working" - What is the occupational position of any occupier who is a retired, unemployed or disabled agricultural worker? If they were previously a stockman (but now are employed as a painter/decorator) this means they do not comply with the AOC.
- A dwelling is defined as "any dwelling, including a caravan, housing a farmer, farm worker, forester or similar and protected for such by an Agricultural Occupancy Condition."
- "The locality" - Sometimes an AOC contains a specific locality clause. In our own case, our "locality" was either our own parish or any of the immediately adjoining parishes only. In reality for us, this meant to comply with the AOC, agricultural employment had to be secured within a three mile radius of our house, so this was very restrictive unless we created our own self-employment opportunity.
- "In agriculture or forestry" - I've given the official definition of agriculture earlier in this section, but I'll now point out what may not be

obvious – farmer, farm labourer, dairyman all comply; farrier, blacksmith, farm accountant, garden centre worker do not. Please take advice if you are in any doubt.

- "Resident dependents" - Technically, this can refer to a spouse if they are a homemaker or unemployed, but not if they have an occupation and their income is equivalent or exceeds the other. This would mean that they are not dependent. The wording is again vague, but aged parents, children living in the household, and those either in full-time education or unemployed could be deemed resident dependents. In 2015, The Court of Appeal considered the definition of a "dependant" in the context of AOCs. In *Shortt v Secretary of State for Communities and Local Government*, the court found that the word "dependant" was not just related to financial dependency. In this case, the family lived in an AOC dwelling and the wife was the agricultural worker who ran the farm, which was operating at a loss. The husband worked elsewhere and the family was dependent on his income. The court held that the definition of "dependant" be widened to include a husband or wife who was not financially dependent on the other, and so the husband was held to be dependent on his wife for the purposes of the condition. This has serious implications for anyone considering non-compliance as grounds for removal of the AOC.

Then in August 2004, the UK Planning system was overhauled somewhat. Planning Policy Statement 7 (PPS7) replaced the old Planning Policy Guidance 7 (PPG7), in

ENGLAND ONLY, which for NEW applications meant that you could now apply for a dwelling if you could prove a "rural based enterprise", rather the very strict agriculture or forestry range of activities. In Wales, TAN6 (Technical Advice Note) is still the recognised authority (basically the same as the old Annex I of PPG7).

Scotland shared the same planning law with England & Wales until devolution and then introduced the Town and Country Planning (Scotland) Act 1997. The attitude to small, local development in Scotland is far less strict than that in England. In fact there has been a degree of sympathy for the establishment of smallholdings, hutting and the creation of new crofts. Of note also, is the intention of the Scottish Government not to limit retrospective applications, but to rectify genuine mistakes in applications. You have to read between the lines here a little, but this basically means that moving-on, building and rectifying are more leniently considered. Planning Aid for Scotland can assist in helping individuals understand and work with the Scottish planning system **www.pas.org.uk**

Enforcement is broadly the same legally in Scotland as it is in England and the statutory periods for limitation are also the same as in England; four years for operational development or change of use to a single dwelling house, and ten years for breaches of planning control. Again, you can also apply for a Certificate of Lawfulness in Scotland as you can in England, and a general reading of applications to remove AOCs shows that there appears to be a more sympathetic attitude in Scotland.

So, the *old*, fairly standard condition of dwellings built prior to August 2004 in the UK, "tied" a dwelling to agricultural use by a farmer, forester, horticultural grower or anyone who last worked as such, or their dependents. The *new* version allows for "rural based enterprises", but does not define this.

The PPS7 Annex A states however, that "the enterprise itself, including any development necessary for the operation of the enterprise, must be acceptable in planning terms and permitted in that rural location". This *could* mean a wide range of activities or businesses given planning permission, to be pursued in the countryside. In practice there has to be a perceived essential link to the use of the countryside. So, in addition to the previous existing occupations of farmers, farm workers, foresters and growers, now it is possible to include equestrian centres, bird of prey centres, green burial sites, and traditional charcoal producers and farriers. Catteries, wood processing yards, agricultural contractors are not generally permitted.

If you intend to buy land and apply for permission to build a dwelling, the degree of success appears to depend on a well-planned, professional application, with support from the local community and a good relationship with the local council. This new option avoids the necessity of meeting the financial and functional requirements of the options existing before, but again, please remember, this is a huge financial purchase, and do take expert advice before proceeding. To prevent any confusion, I stress this applies to NEW properties built since 2004 with Agricultural Occupancy Restrictions in place.

So, now that I've explained what an Agricultural Occupancy Condition is, let's look at how you can buy a property with one and develop a rural business to fulfil the constraints.

Living with an AOC can be very stressful, and I can personally attest to this. Alongside the daily struggles of running a home, looking after a family and making ends meet, you have the obligation to fulfil (in our case) the very strict wording of the AOC. When we realised that our plant nursery business was unsustainable, and we diversified, I was aware that we were no longer compliant with the terms of the tie. My stress level increased, as there was always the possibility of an unannounced visit by the Council Enforcement Officer, and then a Planning Contravention Notice and probable Enforcement Notice; or the equally distasteful possibility of someone locally reporting us as non-compliant.

To comply with the wording of an AOC you will have to become an employee of a farming, horticultural or forestry business or set up your own employment as such. There are many diversification ideas in this book to help you ponder, research and perhaps include on your smallholding or rural business. Modern farming and horticultural methods and automation have meant a reduction in staff numbers, and thus fewer available employment opportunities. You could also be a retired farm worker, or a widow or widower of one. The constraints are out of touch with the reality of today. Most agricultural workers could never afford a typical farm worker's cottage on agricultural wages, even with the reduction to take account of the AOC imposed upon it. The post-war stay-at-home dependent wife is also a thing of the past, as most couples now both have to work for financial reasons. Original owners, who previously complied with the AOC, have possibly died or moved into social care, leaving a property to their family that none of them could hope to fulfil and the necessity of raising funds.

Market Testing

It is possible to remove an agricultural occupancy condition by convincing planners that there is no existing need for agricultural workers dwellings in the area. This requires marketing the property for sale or rent, at a price that reflects the limitations of the AOC, (i.e. reduced by around a third of the possible open market price), for a significant period of time (around two years). If, after a rigorous marketing of the property for this time, there have been no reasonable offers or interest, then the district or country council will consider the application for removal of the AOC.

In April 2019 the Planning Inspectorate emphasised that evidence of a robust marketing exercise is essential when applying to remove a condition. This related to an application to remove an agricultural occupancy condition at Sutton Springs Trout Fishery Grounds. The Inspector found that there had been sufficient marketing of the property as it had been consistently publicised online, included in various publications and promoted in mail campaigns. The agricultural occupancy condition was therefore successfully removed. In a contrasting marketing exercise to remove the AOC, which was rejected by the Upper Tribunal in the case of *Rasbridge, Re Cefn Betingau Farm* in 2012, the Tribunal found the applicants' market testing exercise was not sufficiently rigorous, and suggested that the applicant should have offered to rent the property to establish if there was rental value to the land, advertised the property in the specialist farming press, and adjusted the price to reflect general market movements.

The other option is to apply for a Certificate of Lawful Use or Development (CLUeD), if you can prove without a shadow of a doubt that the occupants of the AOC dwelling have been continuously breaching the terms and conditions of the AOC for a minimum period of ten years. Considerable planning and expert advice is required to go down this route. When we started to amass the considerable paperwork, this included statutory declarations for myself and my husband, a partisan neighbour, and a few good friends who lived locally. Tax records confirming income and job status, P60's, P45's, job and training course offers and termination letters of employment also filled the file. Then there were maps of the property, maps of the area, and photographs and a site visit. The application is decided within six weeks, and the cost involved, including the application to the council, is around the same cost of conveyancing for a property.

Planning Permission for permanent dwelling

Anything classed as "development" normally requires planning permission. But there are some forms of development that are automatically allowed without the need for planning permission. This is "permitted development" (PD). The law changes frequently, but a good source of up to date info is Martin Goodall's book, Permitted Changes of Use (October 2015). His website (see page 58) is also excellent. There are two types of development – change of use, and operational development. Change of use involves a material change of the usage of land or a building; an example would be changing use of land from agricultural to mixed agricultural and/or residential. Operational development includes the building, engineering or mining, in, on, over or under the land. This affects the installation of any building or structure, such as sheds, polytunnels, and dwellings on the land.

Interior changes to a building which do not affect its external appearance are not deemed to be development. Using land for agricultural, horticultural or forestry purposes is also not deemed to be development, and this includes stationing *mobile* caravans for agricultural (not residential) purposes. Using mobile structures, (caravans, tents etc) for residential purposes counts as a material change of use, and IS development. Occasional overnight stays in a shed or caravan on your agricultural holding are not regarded as development, but if this continued for weeks or months, then it certainly would be a material change of use, be considered development, and require planning permission.

Whilst it is not illegal for a person to move onto and live on land without permission, should the local planning authority become or are made aware, they may serve you with an enforcement notice. This allows you 28 days to appeal, and will not take effect until and unless you lose the appeal. In this eventuality you may be given from three to six months to leave. Since the introduction of the 2011 Localism Act, most local authorities do now consider imposing enforcement notices sooner than they would have done previously. Cash-strapped councils are cutting back staff, and the planning departments are no different. This doesn't mean the chances of enforcement officers checking up on all and sundry are few and far between. All it takes is a complaint from a neighbour or other member of the public and planning officers are alerted. If your attempt to live quietly and discreetly on the land is then determined as deliberate concealment, then under the terms of the Localism Act 2011, you could be denied a Certificate of Lawfulness on this basis, and the land in question will retain the enforcement notice and thus be devalued.

In practice you would be better meeting with an agricultural planning consultant and determining the best course of action. As discussed above, planning law changes introduced in August 2004 have affected many aspects of rural planning in the UK. Remember that planning in the open countryside has been curtailed and constrained to prevent blanket building on agricultural land and open spaces. But a change to the General Permitted Development Orders in 2015 meant that adaptation and renovation of redundant agricultural buildings for other uses, including housing, became somewhat easier, with the government stopping local authorities refusing permission for such barn conversions on sustainability grounds, and is covered by Class Q development. There is a current plethora of changes to the GPDO at this time and running up to November 2020, which, frankly, are beyond the scope of this publication, so I direct you to the very knowledgeable Martin Goodall, a solicitor with many years experience in planning law.

http://planninglawblog.blogspot.com/

If you are considering building a dwelling house on land in the countryside, you will need planning permission for operational development and a change of use of the land. Be aware that the process is expensive, lengthy and you are not assured of success. There is no definite "formula" for application; each local authority interprets the law differently, and you are strongly advised if you are seriously considering making an application to firstly contact an independent planning consultant and explain fully your idea. The Planning Portal website, **www.planningportal.gov.uk**, has masses of information on many aspects of planning.

To live on the land, you will need to prove a clear, specific requirement to do so. You will need a detailed and convincing business plan, a professional agricultural appraisal of the current and future viability of your land-based business, and proof that it is essential for you to live permanently on-site. Security considerations are not deemed enough, as modern technology means you can remotely check the security via cameras and other surveillance equipment. Animal welfare reasons such as lambing or calving again are deemed temporary activities which do not require permanent occupation. You will need to think more like a planner and justify and prove your need. In the application show them how your business is viable and how it will benefit the local economy. If your supporting statement can also detail the positive social role, environmental benefits and sustainability of the project, even better. Your application file should be detailed and convincing, including a marketing plan for the business, a list of agricultural or teaching activities that will go on there and the positive impact it will have on the local population. Most importantly, explain your requirement for

58

residential use, why the dwelling needs to be the size you propose and also the locational requirement.

Try to anticipate any possible objections from Highways, Historic England, neighbours, Parish Councils, and cover every possible contentious issue. Prior to any site visit, ensure your land is clean and tidy, visually attractive and that any debris heaps or rusting vehicles have been removed.

You may be successful in your application and be granted a time-limited permission, granting planning but for a limited amount of years. This may be acceptable for those planning to live on-site in say a caravan or yurt, but offers no security for those planning to build a house. Of course, you wish to avoid being refused in the first place, and should consider professional consultancy at the very beginning of the process, but if refused, you have the option of appeal, and can put in an amended application or put in a different application.

Plot & Property Assessment

I would begin any search by narrowing down where in the UK you wish to live. This may be decided by examining a variety of factors. You may wish to live close to existing family, you may need to be close to a substantial city or town for a variety of reasons. Your future project may depend on certain climactic conditions, and require a southern or western location. However, some aspiring smallholders can hunt all over the UK for their future home, being drawn by the sea or by stunning mountains, or vast skies of the Eastern hinterland.

Within the UK, most of us are pretty familiar with the local differences in climate conditions. Western and northern Scotland, North Wales and Ireland are wetter, cooler and generally have poorer agricultural land. This can mean cheaper land prices. South Wales, the border marches and south-west England tend to be prone to flooding, but the soil is rich, and due to larger populations, land can be expensive. Naturally the South East, with its proximity to transport networks and cities, is probably the most expensive. There are local climactic microclimates all over the British isles that confound the accepted ideas – Tayside is a perfect soft fruit growing area, Portland, on the south coast, is becoming the British tornado centre, and the South hams can be positively tropical (as can many coastal villages along the Scottish West coast, nurtured by the benevolent effect of the Gulf Stream). In a nutshell, the further south you choose, the more expensive it will be to find a suitable property, and you will have a longer growing season than in the North.

Use this information to reflect on what is more important to you as you search for the perfect location for your rural business. If you wish to set up an artisan food smokery and target the tourist or hotel market, then being situated on the coastal fringes of Scotland, Ireland or Wales might be the perfect option. If growing Christmas trees is your dream, then poorer agricultural land and colder climate might not be an issue and you could benefit from cheaper prices in such areas.

Your property will be subject to the usual searches before contracts are exchanged, but you will want to assure yourself of as many things prior to engaging an expensive solicitor, especially if any findings are a deal breaker. So, are there any public rights of way on the property? This may be an issue for privacy and the security of your family, home and any expensive machinery, but also a biosecurity and animal welfare hazard if you intend to keep livestock. A quick visit to **www.ordnancesurvey.co.uk** may reveal up-to-date footpaths and bridleways (this is not a free service), or **https://footpathmaps.com/**, but you will need to walk the land yourself to assess issues such as vehicle access to fields, width and condition of paths and gates, maintenance and condition of hedges, fences, drainage ditches, etc. Sadly, in this day and age you also need to think how easy fields and gated access are for sheep rustlers (on the increase in the UK) and fly-tippers (fields with gates set well back from the road are favourites, as are dead-end lanes.)

Assure yourself about any restrictive covenants on the land. Common ones include not causing nuisance to neighbours, keeping certain livestock and not carrying on a business at the property. Although these are more common in town and village settings, ensure your solicitor checks, as any of these will jeopardise any ideas of running a smallholding business from such a property. Such covenants can be overturned by applying to the Upper Tribunal (Lands Chamber) for modification or discharge of such restrictive covenants.

Walking around a prospective property with a clipboard might sound a little pompous, but believe me, making notes and taking photographs is the right attitude to take when contemplating a massive and life changing purchase. Hillsides may give shelter to prevailing winds, but can also be dangerously steep to cultivate or for livestock. Valleys are prone to flooding and frost-pockets, and the land may be waterlogged in winter, with restricted sunlight. Fields surrounded by trees may offer shelter to livestock in summer and winter, but for arable cultivation may be nutrient deficient, dry and full of roots. Generally speaking, a view of the vegetation in the land is very revealing. Clumps of rushes indicate a sour soil, poor drainage and possible clay subsoil. How big an area of the property is affected, and has there ever been any drainage? The presence of drainage ditches alongside field boundaries indicates wet soil. You can get an accurate soil test result from small, cheap kits bought from agricultural stores or online.

61

On the other hand, vast, flat fields with no hedges or walls are often prone to wind erosion, and the soil depleted and dry. Where is the nearest running water on the property, and does it run all year? If you see water bowsers parked up in fields on the property, you can deduce the answer. Coastal properties may have a lovely view of the sea, but they are in the path of salt-laden, destructive winds. Wizened hedges or lack of trees are often a good indicator of frequent coastal winds. Whilst traditional arable farming may not be appropriate here, summer camping or caravan sites and winter sheep or beef cattle grazing may be more profitable. Consider any long-abandoned fields, bracken infested areas, insecure fencing and hedging that may require considerable labour and cost to revitalise into useful farming life again.

Whilst you're there, have a look at any neighbouring properties. You'll be able to see what uses they are putting the land to. Sadly, even small pockets of land unsuitable for conventional agriculture are unlikely to be cheap. There is a never-ending demand for such plots for ponies, pigs, storing boats etc, and no such thing as unwanted land. However unpromising a plot may first appear, remember that it may be suitable for one of the many diversification projects mentioned further on in this book. The beauty of the UK is that there are so many regional variations, and that consumer power is growing. What may be a disaster in one area may be a roaring success in another.

Pylons, Powerlines and Easements

Your tour of the prospective property may have thrown up issues such as footpaths or rights of way, or indeed appear to be a very suitable property indeed. One thing you may totally overlook is the presence of electricity pylons and power lines and poles. A pylon is a bargaining chip when it comes to negotiating the price of agricultural property, because of the health & safety dangers of operating farm machinery underneath them. There has also been much social comment on the possible health effects on occupants of houses sited within 200m of a pylon, and this is reflected in house prices, which may be affected by as much as 15% .

Most pylons have been sited under annual wayleave agreements (this is effectively a form of ground rental) expressly intended to compensate the landowner for loss of the use of the affected land. Most landowners are unaware that they can terminate and renegotiate these agreements, or claim compensation.

It is also possible to claim compensation against the smaller 33kV type of wooden poles that carry lines across properties. A claim for compensation is not affected even if you were fully aware of the line when you purchased the property, or if the property was built after the installation of the power line, or if you are not even contemplating selling the property. However, if you have claimed in the past then you cannot claim again on the same property.

You must first contact your distribution network operator. This is not your electricity supplier. There are ten across the UK and you can find yours on **www.energynetworks.org**. You can claim directly or employ a no-win no-fee company who will deal with everything for you, for a fee of around 10-20% if you are successful. They will, of course, tell you that they will negotiate a larger amount of compensation than you could on your own, which may or may not be true.

The amount of compensation will depend on the numbers and proximity of the pole and wires, and the voltage carried. It can take up to 18 months to process, requires a surveyor's visit and the appointment of a solicitor, who may be paid for by the electricity company. Although a lengthy process, the compensation can range from a few thousand to tens of thousands of pounds, and thus it's worth having a morning chatting to the variety of helpful companies out there keen to assist you in claiming.

Security & Insurance

Every home requires some sort of security, and rural homes and businesses more so than those in relatively populated areas. You will need to consider buildings and contents, personal security, vehicles and plant machinery, safety of visitors, and possibly product security. Prevention is so much better than cure, so let's make a list of things to be implemented to deter the casual thief or criminal gangs who now target farms and rural properties. You already know how to assess your own home for security, don't you? Have a walk around and think about how you would gain access if you left your keys at work or in the pub. Are there any open windows? Are there any ladders or garden tools lying around to help you? Spare key "hidden" under a plant pot or hanging on a string from inside the letter box?

Once you start to think like a thief, it's pretty easy to work out how you can make small changes and increase your security around your home. When I was young and naïve, I used to leave my handbag and car keys on top of the kitchen table, until I heard from a friend who also did this and had them stolen, alongside her car! Where do you keep your jewellery, cash, bank-cards? These are the first questions you'll be asked in the event of an insurance claim. So, your house insurance will cover your personal items, but what happens if you find your brand new livestock trailer, quad bike, welding plant missing? Take every building in your yard and look at it critically. If someone broke the glass in your tractor shed or forced the door or cut the padlock, would you hear it from the house? Make things hard for the thief. Spend a day replacing screws on door hinges and hasps with bolts (with the nut on the inside). Vulnerable windows can have bars or grilles installed inside. Fit insurance-approved locks to all exterior doors, ground floor and accessible first floor windows, and use them. Alarm systems are discreet but useful, as are CCTV cameras linked to your mobile phone. Remember, if you install CCTV you must display a sign at the entrance to your property, and footage may not be admissible in court.

Crunching gravel paths, squeaky gates, dogs and geese can all give you a warning that someone is snooping around. A dog chained in a yard will make a commotion, but sadly is easy to poison, whereas a dog inside a house or building is harder to silence and therefore a better deterrent. Remember also, that pedigree and working dogs have a high resale value, so ensure yours are microchipped (as the law now demands). Sadly, even mutts have a value to dog-fighting gangs. Floodlights with PIR detectors will light up buildings, yards and entrances and deter all but the determined thief. Heavy duty padlocks may prevent valuable red diesel tanks and oil from central heating tanks being emptied. Padlocks or multiple locks on sheds, stables and tack rooms may prevent expensive saddlery and small power tools going missing. Lock all ladders out of sight in a shed.

With rising prices in livestock, ever more reports of stolen sheep, cattle and even poultry show that everything has a value to the determined thief. Remember, if he's targeted your property, he's not going to go away empty handed. He might even take the gates to your fields if you don't protect them by welding a washer underneath the top hinge of the gate.

Finally, have a think about ground-mounted solar arrays. If you have these, the company doing the installation will have given you a run-down on security, as these costly items are much sought after by criminal gangs. Of course you have perimeter fencing secured with tamper proof padlocks and adequate security cameras, but it only takes a few hours for a specialised gang to remove all your solar panels in a single pickup truck.

One of the first things you will have to obtain on your property purchase is home and contents insurance. For a smallholding or farm, this isn't as simple as simply totting up the rebuild value of the house and assessing what it would cost you to replace the contents. Sit down and work out what cover you need and who is best placed to not just give you the cover, but the service you require. Some items will need to be catalogued separately with photographs, detailed descriptions, serial numbers etc all listed. This is especially the case for farm machinery, trailers, ATVs, and farm vehicles. Ensure you have a secure key safe for all vehicles so you can see at a glance if any are missing. Mark all items with ultraviolet or Smartwater markers. If you have a mortgage, your family may be protected if you die, as part of the mortgage payment covers life insurance.

The next thing to think about is Public Liability Insurance. This is a MUST HAVE for any farm, to protect the farm owner from any possible claims from members of the public who could be injured on your farm, or if you are responsible for damage to another person's property. The reasons for this are clear if your farm or smallholding runs a farm shop, campsite, petting zoo etc, but it also covers delivery drivers (including Royal Mail), contract workers and injuries from livestock. Picnickers, walkers, Jehovah's Witnesses and even that thief could claim if they say they injured themselves on your property!

But what about Employer's Liability Insurance? Everyone knows farming can be a dangerous occupation. The Employers Liability (Compulsory Insurance) Act 1969 states that the DAILY penalty for not having a policy in place is £2,500.

Therefore, if you employ any staff or apprentices, you must have this. Of course, you may need specialist insurance if you teach from your smallholding, or if you are a food or drink producer, but the best place to start is to arrange to have a chat with your specialist insurer. NFU, Cornish Mutual and Towergate are just three who cover rural and farm businesses. Don't be pressurised into buying policies you don't need, and watch premiums at renewal time.

Cutbacks to local police services mean there are fewer Crime Prevention Officers, but you will be able to access information on crime prevention, especially rural crime, via the internet. Get to know your local coppers. Let them know they can pop in anytime for a cuppa. Build a similar relationship with your farm and rural neighbours. Many areas also operate Farmwatch groups.

Chapter 3

Acquiring Skills

I have been fortunate to meet many thousands of successful rural business owners, farmers and smallholders. In the main, they have certain things in common – a sense of humour (trust me, anyone working on the land needs this), self belief, pride in their job and the ability to calmly assess any situation they find themselves in. They have all worked hard to achieve their success and many have made sacrifices to do so. However, when, in the course of researching this book, I questioned them to define their strengths and weaknesses, they all gave me a different answer.

Some candidly admitted that they are terrible at maths and give everything to their accountant, some are fantastic at technology and embrace on-line marketing with enthusiasm. Some are terrific communicators, and could possibly sell sand to an Arab or snow to an Eskimo! The things they have in common are that they are unique, and that there is no single skill-set required to run a successful business.

Personal Skills

By examining your own existing skills you will discover that you are, despite what you think, quite talented. The fact that you are reading this book means you can acquire knowledge through reading, and that you are open to considering new ideas. You may have a bit of life experience behind you and probably have had some exposure out in the working world, so let's sit and examine the skills you DO have.

If you own or rent a house, then you probably have some good budgeting and financial knowledge. You know you have to balance your incomings with your outgoings, can budget for car repairs or a holiday. If you have a car you might be able to understand technical manuals and perhaps even service your own car. With a little training you might be able to service a livestock trailer, or possibly a small tractor. Mechanical skills will save garage bills, but also time, and there is nothing more frustrating than having to stop in the middle of a crucial job, such as haymaking or animal movement, because you need to wait for someone else to look at a machine. Of course, having detailed knowledge of machinery and vehicles could mean that you could consider this as a profitable sideline to your main land-based business in off-season. There is considerable profit in servicing and repairing garden machinery, for example, and John, my husband, had a substantial business in horticultural machinery and boat engines. A typical service of a push-along mower took an hour and he charged £50 (in 2017). As his knowledge of machinery grew, he also began to tackle vintage machines.

My own expertise has always been horticulture. I started gardening at the age of nine, learning how to cultivate and propagate plants, basic garden design and growing fruit. I ran a successful gardening business in Scotland, grass cutting, weeding etc, and then designed gardens on a small scale. As a self-employed new businesswoman I had to learn how to do book-keeping and marketing, and signed up for every free course I could get to learn how to do things. When we moved to our smallholding in Cornwall, I took an RHS Level 3 in Horticulture and a degree course in Horticulture, which took up three days of my working week. The theoretical and practical skills I gained along the way helped me to run my smallholding more efficiently and more profitably.

If you have had a career in retail, banking, teaching, hospitality or any working background at all, you have skills you are unaware of. Book-keeping skills, compliance, health and safety, communication skills, IT skills, marketing and selling skills are all really advantageous to any new business. Some skills aren't so obvious. So-called *soft skills* include interpersonal communication, adaptability, innovative problem-solving and time-management skills. Your previous career experience may mean you are happy to embrace new technology, and with the evolving world of agriculture, horticulture, hospitality and retail sectors you'll be completing ever increasing amounts of data, in the form of records, movement forms, computerised machinery and so on. Keeping on top of the latest innovations isn't easy and is time-consuming.

Whilst your old CV or work record might list some of the personal attributes and strengths you have, it doesn't hurt to look at these with the emphasis on how they can fit into your new business plan or project. Start with working out your Strengths on a good old fashioned SWOT analysis. Now, *don't* roll your eyes and push the book away – this is easy! Go pop the kettle on, make a cuppa and come back here.

SWOT Analysis

This simple exercise is to help you, so don't be put off. I explain below how to make a really easy SWOT analysis, and how it will be useful. Keep the sheets and pop them in the folder you will use later when you start to put together your business plan. Yes, a business plan is really useful too, especially if you intend to claim any grant funding. So, a

SWOT analysis is a simple way to look at your strengths, weaknesses, opportunities and threats for any business. Nothing is set in stone, and the document you will produce is a working document, to be looked at again in a few months and then again after a year or so.

- Strengths: What do you do well? What assets do you have? (buildings, staff, equipment etc) What support you have in place?
- Weaknesses: What do you need training in? What's going to hold you back?
- Opportunities: Does your product or service fill a niche in the market? Is there a trend that you can exploit? Can new technology solve a problem for you?
- Threats: Who is your competition? Are there any legal restrictions that will affect your product? Do you have adequate resources to achieve your goals?

Lets start by getting some paper, writing the word STRENGTHS, and then listing them underneath. I'll start you off by listing a couple of mine to give you an idea – good communicator (can talk to all sorts of people all day), good organisational skills (can tell other people what to do), good at managing money (hey, I'm Scottish!). *Yes*, it's a bit tongue in cheek, but people become very self conscious when talking about themselves. Imagine you are at a job interview – tell the interviewer the positive attributes you have. If you have a sensible wife, mum, or good friend, ask them what they think are your positive qualities. They might say you're kind and patient; this is excellent if you have to work with people or animals; or they might say you are methodical and a perfectionist; again, this is great for record keeping and book-keeping.

Hopefully, you will have a few strengths written down now.

If you are struggling, consider if you have to use a computer at all. Word processing or analytical skills and even trawling the internet and knowing how to send emails is a skill! Using a mobile phone and any social media networking is a skill! I joined Facebook many years ago, and actually paid for a three hour course to learn how to use it, basically because my kids wouldn't take the time to teach me. Now I'm reasonably confident in a few social media platforms and I recognise their usefulness in promoting my business, and for meeting like-minded professionals. When I look at my Strengths, I can see a mix of social skills, technological, technical and horticultural skills. You should have a similar spread of your own skills.

So, having looked at Strengths, we will of course now look at Weaknesses; or, as I like to call them, "things I haven't learned yet". So, turn the sheet of paper over and write WEAKNESSES. Under this candidly write what you think you need to improve on. Again, I'll start you off by admitting that when we started our smallholding I never had any animal handling experience other than having the usual domestic pets, so top of my list was farm animal handling. Not everyone has the benefit of a country or farm upbringing, and John and I had a massive learning curve ahead. Second on my list was IT skills. I was confident using programs to write documents or emails, but did not have a clue about setting up a website or internet marketing. So, let's see some words or phrases on the list. You might want to look at training for the paperwork side of things – one day book-keeping or computerised accounting. You may think you need to improve on social media marketing. Maybe the business you fancy starting requires qualifications to allow you to practice – write them down here.

Now, we are all different; this is what makes the world go round, remember? And just because you are rubbish at maths, or you don't feel comfortable talking to strangers, doesn't mean you are going to be a terrible business-person. We all have situations or activities that we are uncomfortable with, but we can work round them. If you're totally unable to do even the simplest accounting, then pay someone to do it, whilst you concentrate on making those artisan goats' cheeses or made-to-measure English saddles or whatever. Work to your strengths (whilst being aware of the weaknesses). Being in business often means having a little knowledge about a lot of things and being a jack-of-all-trades.

You should now have a sheet of paper with some content on both sides of the sheet. That wasn't too difficult, so we are going for another sheet of paper, and continue our SWOT analysis by writing the word, OPPORTUNITIES. Now this is where it gets interesting, and unless you're careful, your clever brain will run away with itself.

So, thinking outside the box a little, you may have an idea for a business that you fancy. By looking around in the locale, you may notice that there is indeed an opportunity for your business. Perhaps the main business in the same field has retired or there was never any provision in your area at all. Demand locally means that customers are demanding your product or services. This is opportunity! If there has been an increase in local housing or population, or a new trend or fad that has led to demand, then someone has to exploit it. Why not you? Sometimes, it's the most random things that you could never plan or foretell. A friend of mine is an adult education tutor, who struggled to get enough numbers to fill her dance classes with elderly students. Then *Strictly* hit the TV screens and she has never looked back. A whole new younger generation want to learn how to cha-cha or tango, and her classes are booming.

The recent Covid-19 pandemic has meant that all sorts of businesses have suffered. Animals still need rearing, crops still need planting and harvesting, and more importantly, customers still need to buy food and services. Instead of wailing and throwing their hands into the air, land-based businesses have pulled their socks up and learned how to market to the internet, and customers have embraced it. Where one market has dried up, perhaps a local restaurant who bought fresh grown salad, another market has appeared: direct sales to the customer who wants local, fresh produce. Internet shopping has never been stronger and as we are now comfortable with it, will there be a return to traditional shopping? The clever business owner keeps communicating with the customer to keep them coming back for more.

With a new understanding and appreciation of food security, many people are now growing their own. And this is a fantastic opportunity if you live near a reasonable population. You can grow fruit and vegetables ready to sell to a whole new customer base, or better still, divide your land into small allotment plots and rent these to customers who want to try growing their own fruit and vegetables. A good website, on-line or socially-distanced courses on the allotment could increase your profits too! So, even a pandemic can be seen as an opportunity.

THREATS is the last of the four sections of your SWOT analysis. If you are serious about starting any local business, you really need to get to know your competition. By this, I mean look at the services they offer, the geographical base they serve. Do they have a good reputation or are they suffered by their customers because they are the only provider in the locale? Is the main threat to your business a lack of capital investment? There are many ways to secure grant funding or training if you require qualifications to enable you to perform your job, such as chainsaw tickets, food hygiene certificates etc. Perhaps the property you wish to run the business from has a covenant preventing any business being run from the location? Remember, covenants can be lifted.

The exercise of completing a SWOT analysis may take you a day or so, but is so useful to make you realise that you actually know more than you thought you did, that you have an idea of what you want to do, and how to do it, and to make you sit and examine the opportunities out there and that threats aren't insurmountable.

Book-keeping and Business Administration

The ability to perform at least basic book-keeping and business administration is essential whatever business you're in. You need to be aware of where your money is at all times. Are you in credit or debit? Which customers have paid, and which need chasing up, and what your money is doing for you. Accurate financial records are necessary for the annual tax return, but also indicate how healthy (or not) your business is. A good, business-like accounting system will also enable you to access grant funding or loans from the bank. They generate confidence in your role as a business owner. Of course, you can use a farm secretary, accountant or farm manager, but there is no substitute for knowing your own financial health, and of course managing your own records is cheaper.

When I first became self-employed I used a simple account book, but in later years, as my business expanded and became more complex, I used Excel on my old computer. I wasn't VAT registered and thus the process was simple enough. I kept a separate bank account for the business and did my accounts religiously every two months. I also visited and made good use of the expertise at my local tax office. Whilst everyone appears to be afraid of The Tax Man, I see these people as a tool to help me. I found out about a one-day course they offered, for new entrants into self employment. I learned loads about what I could claim and how to set up my book-keeping system. Remember that all they want is to ensure you pay the correct amount of tax, and they can, and will, point out where you can save money. You my find it useful to have a look at the useful *Farm Office Handbook* or book one of their one-day book-keeping courses at the Institute of Agricultural Secretaries & Administrators **www. iagsa.co.uk**. You can learn all about setting up accounts systems, VAT and payroll for small businesses, year-end procedures and statutory record keeping.

General office and management skills can be learned at community colleges, Adult Education or privately. Perhaps your accountant would even offer a day training for a fee. When I began self employment, the government offered a business-start up week. Every day covered a different subject – book-keeping, marketing, managing staff. You could pick and choose what you required to learn and access knowledgeable staff to help you if you were struggling with one or more subjects. I like simplicity, but have to say that nowadays basic computer programs can really help you by saving time and money. They can even produce invoices now.

Marketing, these days, has become increasingly internet focussed. The days of having your business name and phone number in the local phone directory are gone. Some sort of internet presence is essential nowadays, and for most businesses a website and social media presence are a way to market, advertise and yes, *communicate* with your existing and future customers. No-one will buy your products or services if they don't know you exist! Since the advent of Covid, internet shopping has soared and many think that customers will not return to their old habits. Naturally, this has limits and people will still need to visit hairdressers, dentists and hopefully markets and farm shops, but shopping for everyday items can now be done anywhere from a mobile phone, tablet or computer.

A good website with lots of great photographs and a way to contact you is essential. It's an expense to set up, with purchasing a good and relevant domain name and a website hosting platform, but these costs should be recouped quickly. Again, you can attend a website making course at your local FE college or Adult education site or through a private tutor. There are many software tools you can use to make your website - Wordpress, Squarespace, Wix and Weebly are only a few to mention. Learning how to add content, photographs and make your website attractive and work hard for you are more skills that it pays to learn. Linking your website to relevant social media is adding another sales platform to your advertising arsenal. Facebook allows you to interact with customers, whilst Instagram and Twitter engage a different sort of audience. You'll need to research which is best for you. Some courses may be funded depending on your financial circumstances, and if not, remember, the cost of a course is a fully tax-deductible expense, and you may be able to access a part-time course whilst working. Some local authority run courses may also be able to provide and pay for childcare.

General and Agricultural Skills

General skills, being somewhat "general", can be learned and accessed in a number of ways, from YouTube, specialist magazines and books, the internet, volunteering at allotments, on farms, from mentors or on specialised courses from other smallholders or farms. Have a look at some of the specialist websites online; the knowledge library on the **https://ahdb. org.uk** website is superb, and **www.ruralbusinessschool. org.uk** is of course, a font of knowledge I was proud to be part of. At one end of the spectrum, you could enrol on a year-long or longer course by a specialised provider such as the world-leading Royal Agricultural University in Cirencester or at one of many locations belonging to the Scottish Rural College in Scotland. If formal courses and qualifications are beyond your requirements, then many agricultural colleges offer day-courses, block release, and online training in a vast variety of subjects. For a range of courses and providers, visit **https://www.aoc.co.uk/land-based-colleges**.

There is nothing to beat hands-on experience, especially before you commit to owning and managing large animals and complicated and expensive machinery. Acutely practical subjects such as animal handling, welding, bee-keeping, butchery, fencing or even using working horses on the farm are best learned from specialists in their field, usually via bespoke training courses. An experienced, patient trainer is essential – look for recommendations or endorsements, check they are properly insured and that the course or training meets your needs.

Training providers in somewhat specialised crafts or services can be difficult to locate, but smallholding groups and clubs, agricultural colleges and specialist magazines or social media pages may provide such courses or leads to appropriate trainers. In Devon, for example, **www.devonsmallholders. co.uk** is run by members and has a dedicated training and mentoring section. For a small annual fee you can access cheap training and be put in touch with more experienced smallholders who can assist you. Of course, there are similar clubs and associations all over the UK, with varying levels of training available. You could also attend livestock shows and big Agricultural Shows and meet many helpful farmers, smallholders, growers and craftspeople there who can point you in the right direction.

Rural skills training is also offered by organisations such

as Lantra (**Lan**d **Tra**ining), who, since the Coronavirus pandemic now offer a variety of remotely delivered training courses, and an online end of course test. Lantra training covers the whole of the UK and is a leading provider in skills requiring qualifications; for example, they offer certificated courses and assessment to enable you to be fully compliant in certain sectors, such as chainsaw, weed application and pest control to name but a few. If your business intends to use dangerous machinery, chemicals or carry out activities such as removing trees etc, you will find that a prerequisite of insurance cover is that you have obtained the correct qualification and that it is renewed as required.

Another general skill I would absolutely recommend to you as a smallholder, farmer or rural business person is to obtain a First Aid certificate. For lone workers or if you are remotely working, it is essential that you have basic first aid knowledge. If you employ staff, volunteers or students on site, you really must have the correct training and a first aid station and policy in place. Check your local agricultural college, F.E. college, Adult Education or even council offices for the First Aid courses in your area.

Specialised Training

Specialised training; sometimes literally in the nuts and bolts of your business, is best provided by fellow smallholders, who generate additional income by sharing their wisdom and experience with those who wish to learn new skills. You, in turn, may, join this increasing band of educators, adding a new string to your rural business bow. Sometimes, in order to learn a particular new skill or craft, this is the only way to learn specifics pertaining to your business model. For example, for me, as a cider maker at Spotty Dog Cider, I had to learn arboriculture and orchard management, the process of cider making itself, learn about liquor licensing, excise duty, labelling and trading standards, then about marketing, social media and add to my growing knowledge of book-keeping and record keeping. And that was just ONE strand of my smallholding business. A combination of acquiring knowledge from books, short courses, speaking to relevant government departments, and then approaching mentors within the industry itself was the way forward. You are unlikely to find a one-stop-shop to learn everything at the same time.

For me, the main provider in this area of expertise was the Cider and Perry Academy at Hartpury in Gloucestershire (**www.cider-academy.co.uk**), although I also learned lots from my local Trading Standard department, Environmental Health Department and from experienced orchard keepers. There are many orchard groups in the UK who offer courses on pruning and orchard management, especially in the main apple growing areas, and even offer milling and juicing equipment hiring too. I was previously involved in one such group in the Cornwall/Devon border, and can recommend them as good places to gain insight on the juicing experience and in growing and sourcing local varieties of apples, as well as other fruit trees.

Many rural-based businesses, especially land-based businesses, know that welding skills are one of the most sought-after skills you can have. Whether you are repairing a gate, part of a trailer or other agricultural machinery, having the skills to undertake your own on-site repairs is a real bonus. An inverter ARC welder allows you to work from a generator if you have no access to electricity. Of course, you need to be able to use a welder safely and competently. Many agricultural colleges offer short non-qualification courses on welding; for example, Duchy College, in Cornwall, is offering a one-day Agricultural Welding for beginners, which covers health and safety and the set up and use of various types of MMA (ARC) welding sets. Other providers offer short courses on gas welding, MMA (stick) welding and MIG welding. There is an article in the appendix in the rear of this book that you may find helpful.

Learning as a Volunteer

One method to acquire hands-on experience or training is to offer your time as a volunteer or helper. Whilst initially, this may seem like a burden to the smallholder, however, you can emphasise that whilst you may not know the skills required for lambing (to take an example) you can certainly be an extra pair of eyes, and also replenish hay or water and replenish bedding in pens. By making the offer of help attractive, you are more likely to be accepted. When I was planning to keep sheep, I volunteered to help with lambing at a tenant farm with a flock of 600 ewes. At first there was much scoffing at how, as a middle aged woman with no experience, I would deal with the very physical business of lambing. After a few nights, they appreciated that I could carry water, sterilize and re-bed used pens, replenish the mangers with hay, and bottle-feed any orphan or smaller lambs. I soon learned how to correct presentations and deal with simple problems. I turned up on time for every shift, and this allowed the real staff to go home, have a proper dinner and perhaps a bath and a nap. Soon I was trusted to work entire shifts alone, with the back-up of my mobile phone in case of real emergencies. I returned the following February, and learned more lambing skills, assisting in difficult births, mothering-on rejected lambs, and tailing and vaccinating. When I had to remove a dead and rotting lamb from inside the ewe, and I was the only one not vomiting, I knew I was deemed worthy.

Some things you can read about in a book or see on a video, but it's not until you are actually in the situation that you will learn. As a tutor in agricultural college, there were classes every year in lambing with a model ewe to try and teach students how to assess and deal with mis-presentations. This, of course is nothing like real life when a ewe may be struggling to free herself, whilst you are armpit deep, trying to get your fingers on a tiny body and correct its position; usually outside, in the dark in the rain.

Some skills must be learned only by carrying them out. Animal handling, lambing, welding, trailer reversing are just a few. There are many organisations where you can volunteer to learn such skills, including Worldwide Opportunities on Organic Farms **www.wwoof.org.uk** and HelpX **www. helpx.net**. These match up volunteers with farms all over the world where the host offers bed and board as well as instruction in exchange for your labour. If you don't have time to volunteer long-term, then contact your local Young Farmers Club or ask your local farmer if you can come along and help sometime. Agricultural students are usually placed on block release to specific placement farms and may need to complete specific tasks in order to gain their certificate or qualification. They learn by a mix of classroom based studies and on-farm training.

If you want to learn nature and environment conservation skills whilst volunteering, you might also try The Conservation Volunteers (formerly known as BTCV). Located all over the UK, TCV offers thousands of opportunities to improve woodland and open spaces, while learning skills such as drystone walling, coppicing, grassland and riverbank management. I myself spent many happy days in Lancashire helping to rebuild a drystone wall, and enjoyed the camaraderie and new skills learned at a relaxed pace.

Internet Learning

Prior to Covid-19, internet learning was seen as a last

resort for many trying to gain knowledge, especially in the agricultural or horticultural sector. However, there was already a wide range of e-learning options of use to busy and remotely located farmers who have used them to their advantage. The Farmers Weekly Academy was a leading name in the field and provided Continuous Professional Development modules with a number of accredited bodies. Sadly, this has ended, and specialised internet learning and qualifications seem to be available in the main from Lantra.

If you fancy learning a little more about keeping financial records and preparing VAT presentations that are acceptable to HMRC, including how to prepare spreadsheets, you could spend a quiet half hour enrolling on an online course (with no assessment) with Lantra (**https://elearning.lantra.co.uk/ category/1#**)

The internet is a treasure-trove of useful (and distracting) information for the rural business person. You can find short instructional videos on YouTube on all sorts of topics from lambing to welding to pruning apple trees. There are dedicated internet sites on specific areas of agriculture, horticulture, forestry, planning, metalworking to name but a few. Online forums such as Downsizer.net, and many Facebook groups such as Celebrating Smallholding offer a community style "place" to share your thoughts, ask advice and even sell your services or products. Remember, the internet is full of individuals only too happy to sound their opinion, and disagreements and heated exchanges can occur, but in the main it's a useful tool.

Compulsory qualifications

Many occupations or businesses in the countryside require compulsory qualifications including the making and selling of food products (hygiene certificates), handling and use of certain pesticides or chemicals, trailer towing, and transportation of animals over certain distances.

If you intend to make any food or drink products including producing meat, meat products, fruit juice, alcohol or honey, you must have early involvement with your local Environmental Health Officer, and they suggest, as best practice, obtaining Food Safety & Hygiene Level 2 for Manufacturing. Whilst, at this time, this certification is not deemed compulsory, it is strongly advocated, alongside a mandatory HACCP (Hazard Analysis and Critical Control Point) plan and Risk Assessment. Your premises will be inspected by your local council EHO (Environmental Health officer) and graded. If your food handling policies and procedures are deemed poor, you may be required to make changes before you are permitted to continue to trade.

For businesses in horticulture, forestry and agriculture, which use pesticides, you must possess a valid pesticide certificate, whether you are self employed, an employee or a volunteer. The foundation module, PA1, has to be obtained before you can sit any further modules (PA2-PA6). The exemption in UK law (known commonly as "grandfather rights") expired in 2015.

If your business requires you to use a chainsaw, it is mandatory to be able to produce a valid and current License to Practice, which used to be called a certificate of competence, (also called a "ticket"), under the Provision and Use of Work Equipment Regulations 1998. The certification is pricey and can be obtained via City & Guilds or Lantra providers. Failure to possess valid certification will invalidate any public liability insurance you have.

Being able to legally tow a trailer on a public road may depend on your age and the weight of the trailer concerned. If you have a full licence issued on or *after* 1st January 1997, you can legally drive a vehicle of up to 3.5 tonnes MAM (maximum authorised mass), towing a trailer of up to 750kg MAM; and you can tow a trailer *over* 750kg MAM as long as the combined MAM of the towing vehicle and the trailer is no more than 3500kg. The MAM is the maximum weight *when loaded* – that is, with occupants and fuel also.

If you wish to tow anything heavier than this, you must pass the car and trailer driving test (**www.gov.uk/car-trailer-driving-test**). This is also sometimes called the B+E test. If you passed your driving test before 1997, check your licence for entitlement to drive a vehicle and trailer of up to 8,250kg MAM. In section 9 of the photocard licence this is categories BE, C1 & C1E (with restrictions on this last category). If you have this, you are not required to pass a special test, although you may wish to undertake some tuition in driving with a trailer, especially as regards reversing.

If you wish to use a trailer or vehicle to transport farm animals, horses or birds in connection with your business over a distance of 65km, you will require an Animal Transport certificate of Competence (ATC). This certificate is widely available from most agricultural colleges and from Lantra.

Accepting Volunteers

In my pre-smallholding days, I learnt a great deal by volunteering to work for board and lodging on established smallholdings, and in time I was able to pass on my experience to other volunteers. When we required volunteers of our own we registered with HelpX, and for two years welcomed people of all ages from all over the world to come and help us on our smallholding. I'm sure we learnt as much from them as they did from us!

As hosts you need to be realistic about your expectations –

you're not getting a worker who will slave all day every day for nothing. Our volunteers put in four days a week from 10-4; in return they received food, accommodation and on-the-job training, and still had time to go and discover Cornwall. For some the curve was steeper than for others: we had two great lads from Spain who had never done any smallholding work, and took a while to adjust to our mealtimes, but we all got there in the end. They helped us put up a building, cut fields with machinery, stacked firewood and even caught and housed a swarm of bees.

Having volunteers is a privilege, and both parties want to enjoy the experience. But there's a serious side too. Scrutinise every applicant and ask for references, especially if you're going to allow them in your homes. Get public liability insurance and provide your volunteers with adequate personal protection equipment. Think carefully about what you need them to do, how long their jobs will take, what equipment they'll need, and what their incentive is. I personally wouldn't work an eight-hour day for someone who treated me like dirt, never said thank you, and didn't offer me lunch or provide protective clothing!

A proper and thorough induction is an absolutely essential start. Introduce yourself and your family and co-workers. Show them their accommodation and make sure they understand how everything works. Feed them. Walk them round the holding explaining the crops, the livestock, what you do, and what you hope they will help you with. If they are young make sure they can contact a parent, and get their parents' contact details from them just in case. Before you shove them out to work, ensure that they know what they are doing and how to do it. Tell them where you are in case they need to ask anything, and tell them when break time is. Even if they are slow, let them finish the job. It will give them confidence, especially if you remember to thank them. Ask them about themselves, what they want to do. Take them to the pub now and again. Lend them bikes so they can get about by themselves. These people are here to learn not just about unfamiliar work, but about an unfamiliar culture – you could be making a big difference to their lives.

CASE STUDY –
Garlic Meadow Smallholding

James & Natalie Hepburn
Garlic Meadow Smallholding
Wales
www.garlicmeadow.co.uk
https://www.facebook.com/garlicmeadow/

James and Natalie began smallholding by buying two chickens for the back garden on the edge of Cardiff, and within a year the numbers had risen to six, and they were hooked. Spurred on by endless River Cottage episodes, they began the search for a piece of land to expand and develop their smallholding lifestyle. On the 14th July 2009 they attended their first ever auction and bought 1.7 acres of overgrown land located about five miles from their house. Neither of them has a background in farming; James is an engineering graduate and Natalie a biochemist.

Issues with living away from the land include visits from the "2-legged fox", but they perceive this is a universal issue for anyone with land or animals these days. Also, time – rather than just walking out the house they have at least a 10 min drive, which becomes an annoyance at lambing time, but they have overcome this to some degree by installing an IP camera in the lambing shed. James still works fulltime for Network Rail, but Natalie gave up full-time employment at the end of 2011, just prior to the arrival of two of their three adopted children, to focus on the expanding smallholding. They now own about 4.5 acres of land over 2 separate sites, rent a further 10 acres and graze an additional 4 acres for people as required.

They continue to keep chickens for eggs for themselves and sell surplus stock. There are also some laying ducks, and some pedigree Dorset Down and Black Welsh Mountain sheep, which they show and sell livestock for breeding purposes, as well as taking some for slaughter and selling lamb boxes. The wool from the sheep is spun and sold as well as sheepskin rugs from the ones turned into meat. There are also 6 goats, who they originally bought to graze scrub land, and they make and sell a range of goat milk soap. The latest additions are 2 gypsy cobs, one has been trained and the other will be trained to work the land mainly harrowing, rolling and logging.

Currently, they estimate around 15% of household income comes from the smallholding, with 50% of that from meat and stock sales with the other 50% from product sales. This is a percentage which will vary over time. With the children still young, they are keeping the business-side small, but as they grow and become more independent, the amount of time they can invest will increase, and thus the income will too. Developing the soap side of the business further and adding new product lines is in the pipeline.

Quote – "Take it steady and remember Rome wasn't built in a day. Have a plan – preferably a short term one and a long term one, but constantly review them and take opportunities as they present."

Chapter 4
Livestock

For many people the sole reason for smallholding or living in the countryside is that they want to keep livestock. They may well have had a life-long hankering for chickens or donkeys, or they may feel that the traditional and sustainable country way of life necessarily implies keeping a couple of pigs, a few hens and some bees. There are some smallholders that keep no livestock at all, because it is harder to make money from livestock than it is from fruit and vegetables, or because they are vegetarian or vegan, but these are in the minority.

And, in this short life we have here on this good earth, money isn't always everything. If you've always hankered for a couple of hens clucking and scratching round the farmyard or to watch a few ducks playing on a pond, then **have** them! Don't go to your grave regretting the hens you've always dreamed of owning.

Let's have a look at some of the things you'll need to consider prior to buying any livestock. Firstly, keeping any sort of livestock, whether its poultry or bullocks, involves long hours, no holidays, and usually regulations and paperwork. Secondly, live animals can be the most contrary creatures, with minds of their own, and unlike rows of peas or fruit trees, frequently rebel against their owners. If your only experience of livestock has been to own dogs or cats, you may feel understandably nervous at the prospect of coercing a reluctant ram, especially if you're small of stature, elderly or physically challenged in any way. In fact, even the most able, strapping novice will find moving, shearing, birthing and general handling of large animals daunting and exhausting. I urge all aspiring livestock owners to volunteer at a farm with the animals you hope to keep, before purchasing. This experience will enlighten you, and your family, and you'll be able to decide what livestock you can comfortably work with.

You also have to come to terms with the fact that, even if you do not plan to keep animals for meat, death, sadly comes to all living creatures, and you as the livestock owner will have to deal with the paperwork, means of death (if not natural) and disposal of the carcass at the end of life. If you intend to keep livestock for food, then this means ensuring the whole family understand and accept that after five or six months, little Snowy will be going to slaughter, to be turned into some delicious chops and joints. Only you can decide whether the end product will justify all the effort, and early discussion with the family will save tears and misunderstandings along the way.

So, having made the decision that yes, livestock is on the list, you will firstly need to obtain a County Parish Holding Number for legal ownership, whether you own the land or rent it.

CPH number or 'Location Code'

If you intend to keep cattle (including bison or buffalo), deer, sheep, goats, pigs or 50 or more poultry or waterfowl, you will need to obtain a County Parish Holding Number, a nine-digit code mainly used to identify and trace livestock from its original point of origin. You must have a CPH number, or as it's sometimes known, a Location Code, even if the animals are kept only as pets.

To obtain a CPH number for land in England contact the Rural Payments Agency on 03000 200 301. In Scotland, contact the Scottish Government Rural Payments & Inspections Division (SGRPID) office (**www.ruralpayments.org**).

You will need the location of your land; the postcode, OS grid reference or land parcel reference number, details about your tenure; i.e. are you the owner, tenant, and your planned activities on the land. If you later obtain additional land, it may be included on your CPH number as long as it is within 10 miles of your main holding (5 miles in Scotland).

The CPH is also the portal to eligibility for subsidies including grants from the Rural Payments Agency and the Forestry Commission, and, in England, countryside stewardship payments.

You will probably also require a Flock or herd number. This is a unique number which will be shown on the official **ear tags** on your animals (where needed). It is stored on a central database to record livestock movements. You can obtain one from your local Animal and Plant Heath Agency (APHA) office, (formerly known as the Animal Health and Veterinary Laboratories Agency or AHVLA). SGRPID will alert APHA when you register for a CPH number – in which case an APHA agent will contact you automatically to get more details to register you for your flock/herd numbers – however, if there is a delay, or you need to register quickly due to deadlines, you may prefer to contact APHA directly yourself once you receive your CPH number.

Remember, when registering for a flock or herd number, you must register your flock/herd to each holding (CPH number) that your flock or herd uses during the year – not just your "home base" holding. Sheep, cattle, pigs and goats need registering. There is no flock number for poultry. For camelids, (alpacas, llamas, etc) there is no current requirement to register for a herd number or to individually identify camelids – however, this may change if a tuberculosis (TB) order comes into place for non-cattle species, so it is wise to keep an eye on developments in this area.

Health, Welfare & other regulations

The health and welfare of farm livestock and the risk of their transmitting diseases of various kinds to each other and to humans are two subjects very dear to Defra's heart, and as a result there are regulations for you to understand and comply with at almost every turn. Fortunately, Defra's Animal and Plant Health Agency is there to help with all the advice and information you will need about flocks and herd books, medicine records, ear-tagging, slap marks and all the other requirements you are expected to follow. Contact your field office at **www.gov.uk/government/organisations/animal-and-plant-health-agency** for more information. This is also the place to notify a suspected outbreak of Avian Flu, Foot & Mouth Disease or any other contagious illnesses on your own or anyone else's holding. This office also oversees animal movement forms, and flock or herd numbers, which must go on animal ear tags alongside your CPH number. For more information on UK government policy see also **www. gov.uk/topic/keeping-farmed-animals** and **www.rspca. org.uk/adviceandwelfare/farm**

Welfare of Animals in Transit

From January 2008 drivers and attendants using road vehicles for transportation of farm animals, horses and birds in connection with an economic activity (i.e. a farm business) for distances exceeding 65km require an animal transport certificate of competence (ATC) to comply with the law. There are many centres who offer the qualification including most, if not all agricultural colleges. Here is a link to the Transport of Animals by road (short journey) test at Harper Adams University **https://www.harper-adams.ac.uk/courses/short-course/course.cfm?id=201015**

Slaughter, deaths and dealing with carcasses

APHA also oversees farm animal slaughter. If you are a small producer and killing to supply your own table, you can do it at home (see the Humane Slaughter Association's website **www.hsa.org.uk**). If, however, you intend to produce meat for sale to the public, you have to use either a licensed abattoir or a licensed mobile slaughterman. See the Food Standard Agency's website here **www.food.gov.uk** for lots of advice.

Wherever you have livestock, you will of course, at some time, also have to deal with the eventuality of death, either from old age, trauma or illness. If you keep poultry or waterfowl, you will need to be prepared to deal with the results of a visit from a fox, badger, weasel or even domestic dogs. Dealing with an injured, terrified chicken can be extremely upsetting, and you may have to make an instant decision between trying to save the creature and ending its misery. I have had two visits from stray dogs, resulting in 15 chickens being attacked. Six had to be euthanized due to extensive injury and/or shock, and you must know how to do it quickly and confidently should you be faced with a similar situation.

The Humane Slaughter Association has information on the

practical slaughter of poultry on its website, which you would do well to look at before the need arises, and I've included a handy "how to" in the appendix in this book. Then you will have to dispose of the carcass. One chicken can certainly be bagged and disposed of in the domestic waste, but numbers of poultry, or indeed larger animals, cannot, and must not be buried or burned on your land. The regulations regarding correct disposal of animal carcasses can be found at **www.gov.uk/guidance/fallen-stock**. They require you to arrange for the animal to be identified, collected and removed by an approved transporter (there is a link on the website) as soon as reasonably practical. If you're lambing, for example, you may wish to wait until you have a number of dead ewes and lambs to dispose of. Temporary storage in vermin-proof bins is allowed if you disinfect after use. The owner is responsible for all the costs.

If you want to know how to kill and prepare a chicken for the oven, then look at the appendix to the rear of this book, where I've detailed how to do this.

Feathered Livestock

Chickens and other poultry are a good introduction to livestock keeping. They are small, relatively inexpensive, short-lived and easy to acquire and keep. You can keep up to 49 birds before you have to register your flock with Defra, which allows you to learn and experiment on a relatively small scale. Poultry keeping is fairly labour-intensive, with birds requiring to be let out every morning and closed in again at night for their own safety. Houses need to be regularly cleaned out, and become filthy in wet weather, and can become infested with mites in hot weather. The used house litter can be composted to produce a great fertiliser around six months later, but you need space and a site far from the house to cope with the large amount of litter if you have more than a few birds. Poultry have to be fed twice daily, but if they are free-ranging they will supplement their diet by eating insects and short grass. A regular supply of clean water is important as chickens can drink up to a litre of water each daily in summer.

If you keep fewer than 50 birds then you can sell surplus eggs direct from the farm gate or at the local market without registering as a food business. However, if you have more than 50 birds or wish to sell to a shop, B&B or restaurant you must register as an egg producer, and follow the rules regarding stamping of eggs, packaging etc. See the regulations here **www.gov.uk/guidance/eggs-trade-regulations**. Bear in mind that although it is free to register, the minutae of detail required must be understood and complied with, and I suggest you sit and work out whether the profit is worth the time and effort involved. For labelling guidelines, contact Trading Standards in your area, not your EHO.

When I started out as an egg producer, with around 100 laying hens, the Egg Marketing Inspector hammered home the point that unless I was prepared to stock thousands of birds, I was never going to make a real profit from selling eggs for eating. He was correct, and after two years, we scaled down, saved ourselves a huge amount of effort and kept small pens of pure rare-breed birds and made considerably more profit selling hatching eggs on an internet auction site.

Poultry require secure housing, an enclosed run if you are going to be away from home or if they are located away from sight; layers pellets or mash, bedding in the form of sawdust or wood-shavings, and also worming at least three times a year with a licensed wormer. Most owners, if they are honest, have a problem with the birds becoming infested with Red Mite and there are a number of treatments for both the birds and their housing. A cockerel is not necessary, unless you wish to breed replacement birds or are particularly keen to hear them crowing (from 2am in midsummer).

Poultry and ducks will happily undergraze an orchard and do little damage to established trees. They will eat insect pests and eat a little of the sward, nitrogenating as they go.

Ducks require a larger house with a larger door. They also require at least enough clean water in which to immerse their heads, and if you cannot provide them with running water they will soon foul any container or pond they use. They will trash the sloping sides of any pond, reducing the natural vegetation with their webbed feet and magically turning it into mud. After a horrific incident where one of the ducks drowned trying to get out of a sunken old bathtub, we replaced this with a plastic baby bath surrounded with pebbles to limit the destruction and the copious amounts of water they use up. Our ducks were Cherry Valley crossed with Aylesbury's, and they were a delight with their antics and happy quacking. They laid regularly and grew quickly, being killed and prepared for the table at 14 weeks. In wet winters, they unfortunately "dibbled" the wet and poached soil in part of the orchard, damaging the roots of some young apple trees, and so needed moving to fresh pasture pretty often. Like poultry, they need protection from the fox, and are a bit silly and slow – hence the expression "a sitting duck".

They will happily (and greedily) eat layers pellets and so we let the chickens out first, and waited ten minutes before releasing the ducks. They can be kept in the same paddock or run as poultry, but ensure you have enough ducks to keep your drake happy (if you have one). One drake to 4-8 ducks is a good ratio; otherwise you may find some traumatised or even injured poultry.

Geese are large birds and need a large area of secure pasture to graze. They like water also, and can be found bathing and submersing their heads just like ducks. As larger and heavier birds, they will muddy the margins of any pond considerably. Grass alone is not enough, and geese can also be fed layers or growers pellets, mixed corn and left to clean up used vegetable gardens. If left for any time in a young orchard they will strip bark from the trunks, and thus severely damage the trees. Three geese will make short work of a half-acre paddock and need supplementary feeding for at least a month prior to slaughter. You also only get one meal from a goose, and when you look at the fact that two lambs raised in the same area will provide you with enough meat to eat lamb once a week for a year, I know what makes more sense to me to keep. Geese also have a well-deserved reputation as guards. They will make a considerable noise if anyone approaches their territory, and can give a nasty and painful bite with a large serrated beak.

Other feathered friends you may wish to consider, include turkeys or quail. There is a small window of opportunity at Christmas for turkey sales, which may tempt someone who can see an outlet at a local farmers market or selling direct from the farm. Free-range, corn-finished premium birds can fetch a good price. Although poultry of all species are prone to a few diseases, turkeys appear to be particularly prone to Blackhead or Histomoniasis. The risk can be lessened by keeping turkeys apart from any other birds or rearing them in barns.

Quail will supply the small eggs so beloved of high-class restaurants and tiny birds, spatchcocked and ready for the oven. Unlike some other European countries, quail are not regularly seen in UK supermarkets, but these birds can offer a market for both birds and eggs if the producer lives near a large and affluent population. With carefully controlled indoor or secure outdoor pens and runs, you can produce birds and eggs for a good part of the year. A female can produce up to 170 eggs. From hatching to laying takes around six weeks, and birds are ready to eat at nine weeks. They do not require a huge amount of space, but do well in secure, vermin-proof, well ventilated but secluded habitats with winter heating.

Guinea fowl are another specialised species who offer a pretty and edible addition to a smallholder's collection and are easy to feed and keep; however, they do not readily take to secure housing, preferring to roost on buildings or in trees, and therefore can be vulnerable to foxes.

For most of the feathered species, worming and keeping a watch on external parasites will be the main health issues you need to be aware of, but Avian Flu is a recurring problem for those who live in coastal areas, where migrating wild birds, such as ducks and geese tend to congregate. Avian Flu is pretty rare in domestic flocks, but you need to be aware of the symptoms of it, and prepared to protect your birds if there is a confirmed outbreak near you. You must keep your flock enclosed in secure housing, which may be an issue if you have large numbers of birds. Any outbreak may affect you if you are keeping birds for egg production or meat sales, and you will no longer be able to call your products free-range if they are in confinement. It's also a notifiable disease, and if you suspect any of your birds have contracted it, you must let your vet know and also contact APHA immediately. Keep all deceased birds in secure bins in case they wish to conduct tests.

Bees

Bees produce so many valuable products and offer a fantastic pollination service that I'm surprised more smallholders do not keep them, or provide sites on their smallholding for local bee-keepers to keep a few colonies. They take up so little space, and only need a warm, sheltered area with varied vegetation so they are excellent in the small, untidy or scrubby areas found everywhere on small farms or at the back of gardens. Crop production is significantly increased by having them located nearby, sometimes by up to a third, and of course, they produce honey and also wax.

Fencing off a small area of perhaps only two square metres will house two colonies in an area away from other farm animals. Horses don't like them and other animals may try to use hives as scratching posts and upset the hives and bees. Face the entrance of the colonies into the sun, unless you are located in a very hot area. They require no work in the winter, apart from a short check of the closed hives' weight to ensure they still have sufficient stores, and from March until early October you need only check them physically once a week to ensure they are happy, have a laying queen and are not expanding too much for the brood box and supers that you have for the colony.

In late August you can harvest your honey from the supers and either store the honey in jars or as cut-comb for sale. Local honey is much prized and can add considerably to your profitability, especially as cut-comb, which, for its weight, commands a higher price than jarred honey. After harvesting you need to treat your colonies against Varroa, which sadly is now present all over the UK. Varroa mites can severely diminish the health of a colony if left untreated, but treatment is simple and relatively inexpensive. Once treated, ensure your bees have sufficient stores to see them through till spring. Asian hornets, once rare in the UK, are sadly now no longer a visitor, but living and breeding in the UK. They are visually different from native hornets with a distinctive orange/yellow face and are voracious predators of honeybees. A bee-guard on the entrance of the hive will offer some protection, as will removing any landing boards on the front of the hive.

You can find lots of information on bee-keeping by visiting the website of the British Beekeepers Association, **www. bbka.org.uk**, and a useful book on the subject is *The Complete Step by Step Book of Beekeeping*, by David Cramp (2015). The late Dave Cushman developed a wonderful website devoted to bees, which can still be accessed at **www.dave-cushman.net**, and if you enjoy watching videos, have a look at the very enjoyable video here, where Charlie Dimmock learns a little about beekeeping **www.youtube. com/watch?v=-fMlJoeEQcA**

Sheep

Most smallholders have a preference for either pigs or sheep, but do not often keep both. Naturally, it's your choice of animal, and you may have a variety of reasons to keep one or the other (or indeed, both). We plumped for sheep, basically because I like sheep, and we didn't have room for both species; although as a cider maker with orchards, it probably would have made better financial sense to go for pigs, but as I mentioned earlier, money isn't everything, and I like sheep.

A stocking density of 6-8 sheep per acre, (all year) is feasible depending on the quality of pasture you can provide, but keeping sheep all year is more costly and labour intensive. The year begins with lambing in early spring; lambing is preferably managed indoors, if you have the facilities, and the lambs are turned outside to fresh pasture as soon as they are thriving. They are not shorn in their first year, but older hoggets, or mature sheep, need their fleeces removed when the weather turns warmer; usually in May. This is a good time for a general health check of the flock. As autumn approaches, ewes are selected for breeding, and a ram, or tup, is put in with them with a coloured crayon or dye on his chest which will indicate which ewes he has served. Traditionally the ram was put in with the ewes on Bonfire night so that lambing wouldn't start until April when the weather was kinder. Modern farmers may introduce the ram earlier to stagger lambing periods, or to take advantage of a better market price, when there is less of a glut on the market.

If you are in the southern counties, you may be able to take three "crops" of lambs in two years, especially if you have Dorsets or Poll Dorsets. So, aim to lamb them in December, then again eight months later and then after the following eight months, and you would be selling those lambs when they reach between four and five months old (from June until August). I can do this here in south west France with Causses sheep, who seem to fall pregnant at the drop of a hat.

Breeding ewes usually produce twins, which can be kept and fattened for four–five months before slaughtering. Ewes can produce lambs from their second year until around the age of six or seven before productivity dips. Different breeds have different characteristics, and prefer different locations. Native breeds, which tend to be closer to "wild" sheep, can be harder to keep enclosed, and are, on the whole, less docile than more commercial breeds. They are best suited to upland, poor grazing in challenging locations, such as coastal or mountain areas. They include breeds such as Castlemilk Moorits, Shetland sheep, and Herdwicks. They produce smaller carcasses and their wool is much coarser. Larger, traditional breeds, such as Suffolks and Border Leicester are good breeds for large meat carcasses and thrive on most locations in the UK from the Southern Uplands of Scotland to the Home Counties. Where you enjoy warm weather, sheltered grazing and decent pasture you would be better to look at commercial breeds such as Beltex or Texels to produce good lean carcasses, beloved of supermarkets, or downland breeds, such as Dorsets, Poll Dorsets, Ryeland or Shropshire sheep. Their wool is prized for turning into yarn, and of course, the meat is also delicious. They also seem easier to domesticate and rarely yearn to escape.

Sheep require shearing, (unless they are Wiltshire Horn or Easycare Sheep) in early summer for welfare reasons, and many need supplementary feeding over winter with hay or even pellets if the winter proves to be a hard one. Raising lambs as a high-value product worked for us. We did not possess enough land to keep our own flock of sheep year-round, and keeping bottle-fed or cade lambs from March until October kept the pasture down, fertilized the soil, and when slaughtered filled our freezers with good, home-produced, grass-fed lamb. There was no shearing, winter feeding, nor rams or lambing to arrange. In Cornwall, we kept two lambs on half an acre from March until October, where the pasture was rich; and here in France we keep two lambs on an acre of poorer, drier pasture from March until July, when the pasture disappears in the summer heat. One lamb has always been for our own use; the other, when it comes back from the butcher, is sold. It is an efficient way to generate income and I get the joy of bottle-feeding and cuddling.

You have to be aware that there are some diseases that can be transmitted from sheep to humans, including chlamydiosis, toxoplasmosis, listeriosis and Q fever. ALL are very rare in sheep and very, very rare in humans. If there is a possibility you could be pregnant, then you must avoid delivering lambs, do not milk ewes, avoid contact with live or dead newborn lambs and the afterbirth, or contaminated bedding. Wash all clothes worn during lambing time separately.

Similarly, if you employ female staff you have a responsibility to minimise the risk to female staff who may be pregnant, members of their family and visitors to the farm.

103

Goats

Goats are increasingly popular in the UK, as an option for both meat and dairy production. They can be the Houdinis of the animal world though, so excellent fencing is required; and the uncastrated males have a pungent, lingering odour. You will need shelter for them as their coats are not waterproof, and prolonged exposure to poor weather will make them ill. If you decide to keep dairy goats you'll also need a small milking parlour, and a sheltered barn for kidding. They will destroy an orchard but do very well on rough, stony ground, as they are browsers rather than grazers, and your stocking density per acre should be around six to eight animals. They are good to follow on after cattle or sheep, and eat what they ignore.

There are a number of breeds available in the UK, including Toggenburgs, which are good dairy goats, producing milk for two to three years after kidding, or Boer goats for meat production. By using a Boer billy on dairy goat nannies you can produce kids that can produce good meat carcasses, whilst still getting milk from the nannies. Many smallholders and small dairy outfits make a good profit from goat's milk, which is easier to digest than cow milk, and from the many varieties of cheese that they can make. The meat is being increasingly valued, and is a good seller in the UK, and in demand from cities with large Asian and Caribbean populations. Find out more at **www.britishgoatsociety.com**

Pigs

Pigs can be an ideal animal for the smallholder. They can clear scrubby, overgrown areas and manure it as they go, eat vegetable waste from the vegetable garden and orchard (in addition to proper pig nuts), and will provide you with lovely meat. Be wary about stories about certain breeds of pigs being safe to release into an orchard, though. All pigs dig, and will destroy an orchard if kept there for longer than it takes to eat the windfalls. Electric fencing at 6" and 12" (checked daily) and dry movable housing are necessary. They are natural woodland beasts, so fencing off part of a wood is ideal, but they will quickly transform normal pasture into a scene from World War I. They're social animals, so you need to keep at least two, and unless you have a very large market for your meat, a couple of weaners of the same sex at any one time will probably suffice. Whether you choose gilts or boars is a matter for personal preference, and stories of boar taint seem to be exaggerated, according to all the pig keepers I've spoken to. Oh, and just a heads-up for anyone considering micro-pigs – there is no such thing! All pigs are small as piglets, but they all grow into large pigs.

You could stock as many as six weaners an acre for a period of around five to six weeks, with additional feeding, as long as you are prepared for total clearance of the land, which will need to be left to recover significantly. You could try a three-year rotation, planting a third of your land with roots such as turnip and a third with legumes or maize, with the final third as pig pasture. The Green Pig Project, in conjunction with Defra, conducted a survey showing that native legumes provide adequate protein and nutrition, when used as a feed additive, and this reduces dependence on expensive and unethical soya mixes.

Pigs will be ready for slaughter as early as four months old, depending on feeding and intended use, and used to be more economical to keep than lambs. Rising feed prices and restrictions on using leftover human foodstuffs mean this is no longer the case, unless you intend to grow your own feed crops. Strict rules on feeding kitchen scraps or catering waste have been introduced to limit the introduction and spread of notifiable and deadly diseases such as Swine Fever and Foot and Mouth Disease. If you think pigs might be an ideal choice for your smallholding, farm or rural business, find out more here **www.britishpigs.org.uk**

Cattle

A larger smallholding or small farm can support some breeds of cattle in small numbers. Dexter's, Belted Galloways and Shetland Cattle are just a few of the more suitable breeds, with the Dexter often hailed as the ideal smallholder's cow, despite it being considered a little lively. You could stock smaller and hardier breeds of cattle at a ratio of one adult per acre, but may have to house and feed in winter, to prevent poaching of the ground in wet areas. Housing is also required if animals are calving, and a cheap camera located in the barn and sending a feed to your computer or mobile phone will alert you of any progress. Killing meat animals at 20-24 months will produce around 150-220kg of meat, depending on the animal and the butcher. As with lamb and pork, there is a growing market for local produced beef, and some simple processing of the cheaper cuts will increase sales too.

A good way to enter ownership is to buy an in-calf cow with a youngster at foot. This way you have company for the cow and a supply of meat to grow on. With good management you could supply yourself with milk and meat for many years. In winter, cattle need about half a small bale of hay each daily, and any root vegetables you can supply.

Cattle are also prone to contracting tuberculosis, and testing is mandatory and frequent, although this is dependent on where you live in the UK. If the test proves that the animal is a reactor (positive test), or the test is inconclusive, then that animal must be isolated from the rest of the herd, and removed from the holding for slaughter. Your smallholding or farm will have movement restrictions imposed if you have other cattle or camelids (alpacas), and after your reactor animals are slaughtered, you will have to clean and disinfect areas of the farm. You may be able to claim compensation for the animals if they have the correct ear tags and passports, but if it was a prize bull or carefully bred breeding cow, this will fall short of the devastating loss to a dedicated owner. Compensation rates depend on the animal's age, sex, pedigree status, and whether it is a dairy or beef animal. Until there is an effective and safe vaccine for combating tuberculosis in cattle in the UK, thousands of farmers will continue to face stress, hardship and financial loss through infection. It will be of no surprise to readers that this, together with a meagre profit margin on milk sales, has resulted in many UK dairy farmers giving up and farming in other ways.

Alpacas

There is considerable debate about the subject of alpacas or Camelids, in the UK farming and smallholding arena. Like Marmite, it appears you either love them or hate them. I'm afraid I'm sceptical of their contribution to profitable smallholding, unless you keep them as pets or as a trekking option. There is no real market for their meat, and collecting the fleece isn't an easy job. And yet, people seem to love them. They need to be kept in a small herd and are expensive, and around four or five per good quality acre seems to be a good stocking density. They can be out-wintered, but if you plan on keeping them for good quality fibre, then providing winter housing will protect their fleece. Summer shearing will produce three to five kg of fibre annually. Shearing normally requires at least two people and animals are laid on one side and tethered by the feet to prevent the animal moving and also to prevent kicking. When one side has been sheared the animal is rolled over and the other side sheared. Obviously regular handling will ease any operations such as shearing, foot trimming or teeth trimming (again a regular necessity).

There appear to be over 45,000 alpacas in the UK, so clearly they have a considerable following, and small herds are frequently kept alongside sheep or poultry, where their presence is said to deter foxes. In their native South America fox-type predators do target cria (baby alpacas) and wild adult alpacas will chase and trample them to death if they can.

The British Alpaca Society has relevant information for aspiring owners on their website, **www.bas-uk.com**.

Hedging and fencing

Fences and hedges that will keep your stock in, and unwanted visitors out, are expensive capital items that have to be constantly checked and maintained and regularly replaced. Even tanalised fence posts will only last 7-8 years. Nevertheless, boundary protection is important and should never be neglected since the consequences can be dire.

Hedges are certainly more appealing visually, and harbour a wealth of insects to feed wild birds such as sparrows, but they do need to be thick and spiny right from the ground up. If a hedge becomes gappy at the bottom it can be cut and re-laid to make it stock-proof. The new growth will shoot vertically from stems that are almost cut through horizontally and then laid almost flat. You might be advised to entrust this highly-skilled task to a professional, but there are detailed instructions and a video at **www.woodlands. co.uk** . A well-laid boundary hedge will only need a light trim of the sides and top for the first ten years or so before a substantial overhaul is required.

We cut and laid our mixed blackthorn and hazel hedging and,

although it took a good 18 months to recover, it certainly thickened and rejuvenated it. It also recovered two metres of extra land inside the boundary. If you have a blackthorn hedge clean up carefully, and burn the brash if you can in situ – we had two car tyres requiring replacement immediately after we cut and laid the 100 metre long hedge.

A dense hedge is an effective windbreak, sheltering livestock from the icy blast and helping prevent dry soil from blowing away in hot spells. It also provides a whole ecosystem for many useful plant varieties: sloes for gin and vodka; hazels for nuts, pea-sticks and walking sticks; damsons and bullace for wine, pies and liqueurs; and elder for both blossom and berries, which make fine wines and a lovely light elderflower cordial.

Many companies stock mixed native hedging species, which you can purchase to gap-fill or create new hedging, safe in the knowledge that no poisonous species are included. Stagger planting and protection with spiral protectors will allow the best possible chance for a thick hedge to establish itself.

Fencing can be expensive but it's worth doing properly. Good fencing certainly makes good neighbours. There are a few alternatives to consider –

- Post and rail – attractive and expensive, not really adequate to keep medium sized animals secure.
- Post and wire – more effective animal control, cheaper than above, but beasts will still try to force a head through.
- Post and mesh – effective if constructed carefully, with decent posts and mesh stretched through top and bottom wires. A single strand of electric fence 15cm from the bottom will deter pigs from trying to "nose" under the

mesh.

- Electric fencing – expensive but versatile. Can be moved around and run from either mains electricity or solar. Needs frequent checking and a little maintenance.

CASE STUDY – Mike & Ellie Paddock

Hitch in Farm
West Devon
www.hitchinfarm.co.uk
https://www.facebook.com/hitchinfarm

Mike and Ellie are both 30 years old now and met in 2014, when Ellie undertook a horse-logging apprenticeship, having previously worked in ocean conservation. Mike has been working with horses since he was 16, and prior to working as a horse-logger, he was the head horseman to HRH The Prince of Wales. The decision to start a business was made in 2014, and the land purchased the following year.

Neither are from farming backgrounds. Mike grew up in Cardiff and Ellie had an international upbringing. A family inheritance meant Ellie could raise the finance required to purchase land in 2015. With prices very high in the area there were living they chose West Devon, where they bought 35 Acres.

They have 2.5 acres for crops, cut approximately 10 acres of hay, and 2 acres of woodland. The rest is grazing for horses, cattle and a flock of 20 sheep. At this time, they live on-site and are navigating the planning system for future development, to make their life a little easier.

The majority of their income is generated from training horses for others, with a good percentage from training courses on-site, and the rest from selling vegetables, lamb, pork and sheepskin rugs etc. They also do contract logging and bracken rolling, and some shows and demonstrations. They work exclusively on their smallholding and make a fairly decent income.

Their biggest issues are spreading themselves quite thin, and struggling to find staff, as the work is so specialist. But they have used lockdown to reassess what they are doing and have rewritten their business plan.

In the next five years they would like to become more self-sufficient and explore more permaculture and silvopasture options, although to be fair, they admit they are pretty close now to self-sufficiency, as they produce our own veg, soft fruit, meat, milk and eggs. They would like to develop their orchard, and also to start beekeeping.

Quote – "Get decent fencing, and learn how to fix it yourself. If you can't keep your stock in you can't do much!"

Chapter 5
Food & Drink Production

Producing food or drink from your smallholding, farm, allotment or garden is perhaps the most obvious way of saving money or making an income from it. Taking into account the fact that everyone's location and circumstances are different, the diversity of possible projects is so vast that there will be something that suits you. Even those who do not have any land to speak of can forage from hedges, public spaces, and the seashore; and there is always adding value to raw food ingredients which you can then re-sell at a profit. Small gardens and allotments can produce substantial amounts of fruit and vegetables to make jellies, jams, juices, chutneys or chilli sauces, and can house a colony of honeybees for honey.

Whatever project you decide, please do look at the costs involved, and do your sums carefully. If you treat even the smallest project as a business, and factor in your time, cost of packaging and labelling, transport and, if selling at a market, pitch fees, you will soon see if the time and effort involved is actually profitable. Also, try and spread your risk and your market share by offering more than one product line, and ensuring that what you are selling is a high value item.

In this chapter, I have avoided discussing cider or apple juice and have devoted a whole chapter to orchard products further in the book. Do have a good read; an orchard is literally a place where money really does grow on trees!

Eggs

I'll begin with egg production because it's usually the first enterprise most smallholders or large garden owners with a few hens begin with, when they have a surplus of eggs, and as such is entry-level into food production from the land. I also have fairly extensive personal experience with this as I was registered as both an egg producer and an egg packing station at my smallholding in Cornwall.

On a small scale, it's one of the easiest ways to make a bit of pocket money from your hens, and requires nothing more than a sign at your gate with the price on it, or you can take them into your work and sell them direct to work colleagues, or sell them door-to-door. You cannot claim that the eggs are "free-range" or "organic" unless you have complied with the particular regulations, and in the case of organic, you must have prior registration for organic status (not free).

At this level, selling directly to the end-user, there is no regulation involved, but you are never going to make much money. If you look at it as a way to sell surplus eggs, and to recoup some of the costs of feed and bedding, then good luck. A box of six eggs can be priced at an average of £1.50, but as a group of four laying hens will produce (in summer) around 24 eggs weekly and fill only four boxes, don't put a deposit down on that luxury yacht yet. If you then decide that you wish to increase your flock size to increase your egg sales, there are some things to think about.

Having a flock of 50 or more hens means you must register your flock with Defra; a relatively quick and pain-free online application. In fact, you can legally keep up to 349 birds and sell their eggs direct to the end consumer before you have to register as an egg producer.

However, the minute you start selling eggs *indirectly*, you have to consider the legal requirements. Selling eggs from a stall at a market requires registration with Defra, and registration as a food producer with your local council's Environmental Health Department, and eggs must be stamped with your producer number. Selling eggs to a middle-man; i.e. to a shop or restaurant, or B&B (even if this is your own B&B) means you need to be a registered egg producer, an egg-packing station and be registered with the council as a food producer. Again, eggs must be stamped with your producer number, and your egg box label with your packing station number. You will also have to contact Trading Standards locally, as to their requirements for what you must include on your egg box labels. More information and how to register to sell eggs can be found here **www.gov. uk/guidance/eggs-trade-regulations**.

You will need to adopt the mind-set of a business, and realise that hens are a "crop". To make a decent return you will have to select commercial hybrid birds at point of lay and replace them around 18 months later, as production levels start to drop. What to do with "spent" birds is an ethically sensitive subject, so you could try to privately re-home them, or contact the British Hen Welfare Trust, who re-home ex-commercial laying birds (**www.bhwt.org.uk**).

Having large amounts of birds will naturally increase soil erosion around housing, increase the incidence of rodents, may increase smell and flies, and probably present a problem in controlling the dreaded Red Mite, which will adore a chicken shed stuffed with a high density of hot little hens. You must take the trouble to sit down and work out if the possible profit will wipe out the time, effort and expense incurred. Factor in large housing costs (and possible permission from planning), pest control, feed, water, packaging, labelling, and staff costs. Worming must be conducted routinely; you must have a dedicated packing area with hand-washing stations, and the equipment necessary to check egg weight and quality prior to packing. Then there is storage and refrigerated transport.

I was an egg producer and packing station for two years before I finally faced the facts that I would need to own a flock of at least 500 birds before I would break even, let alone make a profit. Although at the time the EU allowed a stocking density of 1000 hens per acre, this factory style production was not what I wanted to do on my smallholding, so I ran the project down.

As I still wanted to keep chickens, a more viable option for me was to concentrate on small breeding sets of pure-breed hens. Instead of selling the eggs for eating, the eggs were instead kept to sell, via an online auction site, to dedicated breeders and fanciers. The price for six eggs climbed from £1.50 to up to £16 at the start of the season. Of course, reputation is key. You must have healthy, well bred birds true to the breed standard, postage must be quick and packaging robust enough (polystyrene egg boxes are the best method) to survive delivery to the end purchaser. Living in the far south-west meant that light levels increased sooner than other parts of the UK, and a test hatch could be conducted in early February and sales commencing mid February, before my other competitors with similar good reputations. With five groups of popular breeds, I was soon making more than enough to pay for their feed, and all the other ancillaries involved, and still had eggs for my own family's use.

If you fancy a little variety, keeping ducks or quail will also provide eggs, and a ready market for eating eggs. With ducks, the going rate is roughly the same as hens' eggs, but the season is shorter. You could always breed your own and raise some for meat, or again, sell fertile duck eggs for hatching.

One last thing to think about is what to do with all that spent bedding and manure. At a rough estimate 50 hens could produce over 2 tonnes of manure annually, so rotating pasture is necessary, not just to reduce the manure burden on the soil, but also to prevent build up of worms and parasites on the pasture. If you keep smaller quantities of hens, then rotating the house or coop around the garden keeps the grass from being destroyed, and indeed, siting on the vegetable patch will soon remove any weeds, whilst the hens increase the fertility of the soil. Chicken manure and bedding can be composted or dug into the ground in winter. Use as a top dressing before ploughing can also add vital nutrients and organic matter into crop fields, inside polytunnels or glasshouses or no-dig beds (have a look at Charles Dowding's website, **https:// charlesdowding.co.uk/**). An average tonne of poultry litter contains 25kg each of nitrogen and phosphate and about 20kg of potassium, so is a fantastic and sustainable product which can be used in a number of ways and settings, or you could even compost it, then bag and sell it.

Cheese

Cheese making is growing in the UK and is especially popular amongst diversifying and ex-dairy farmers. They already own a lot of the equipment required, are used to unsocial hours and realise they can turn relatively unprofitable bulk milk into a high value artisan cheese. Many stick to owning cows, but many move to owning sheep or goats for cheese-making. The animals are easier to manage and can be stocked at a higher density than cattle, surplus offspring can be reared for meat, and there is none of the heartbreaking tuberculosis testing or slaughter.

Of course, setting up as a cheese maker will incur some substantial capital investment. In addition to the housing, land and equipment associated with your animals, you will also need a milking parlour, dairy, milk tanks, cheese vat, pasteurisation equipment, storage and packaging equipment. A really useful guide (although out of date as far as pricing is concerned) with lots of technical information was published in 2009 by DairyCo, **https://www.scribd.com/ document/241916732/On-Farm-Small-Scale-Cheese-Making-a-Beginners-Guide**. Of course, equipment can be purchased second hand, but estimating between £12,000 and £20,000 will give you an idea of the investment required. Some cheese-makers buy in supplies of milk and avoid the necessity of owning and managing animals, and you can try cheese-making yourself on courses offered by many small cheese makers including **https://ribblesdalecheese.com/**, **https://wildescheese.co.uk/collections/cheese-making-classes** and also **www.highwealddairy.co.uk** .

Once you have mastered the art of cheese making, and secured your capital investment, you'll have to decide what sort of cheese you want to make. This will be affected by how quickly you'll want to sell, as hard cheeses take considerably longer to mature than soft cheeses; and a nine-month wait before you can present your cheese to the market will necessitate a larger bank balance, and therefore a slightly increased risk. Market research is also key. You must define what the best selling cheese products are in your area, assess the demand, and pinpoint any gaps in the market for your product. The artisan cheese market is a serious one, and the packaging and marketing of your product must reflect this. Whilst a novelty cheese may sell as a one-off joke, it's unlikely to get you any regular demand. Target the local delicatessens, farm shops, restaurateurs and the foodies who flock to farmers markets, and especially have an attractive online shop on your website. **https://www.thecourtyarddairy.co.uk/blog/**

Other Dairy Products

As part of the dairy industry process for making butter, cream and cheese, rennet (an enzyme) is added to milk to separate milk into whey (about 15%) and curds (about 85%). Whey is normally sold off to baby milk manufacturers or for manufacturers of body-building supplements. As a small producer, the smallholder could simply spray it (diluted) onto land as a soil conditioner (it's rich in protein), or add to animal feed in winter. However, whey can also be used for the production of cheeses such as ricotta and as a substitute for water in bread-making and cake making, adding to milkshakes and smoothies, soups and stocks. There are actually two types of whey: one produced by the adding of rennet to milk, called sweet whey, and the other produced by adding lemon juice or vinegar to create an acid whey. I won't delve into the mysteries of whey in this book, but just search the internet to while away many hours discovering vast amounts of uses and recipes.

Other dairy products that are more popular, profitable, and enjoy a faster turnover than cheese are yoghurt and ice-cream. Ice-cream is an industry currently enjoying a huge growth in sales in the UK, especially in times of recession, and offers the artisan producer a good living if it benefits from a unique USP (unique selling proposition) and excellent marketing. The market is vast and covers organic, Italian Gelato, yoghurt ice creams and high-fat premium ice cream. Using the traditional method, 10 litres of ice cream costs around £17 to make and can sell as single scoops at around £1.50 each, thus producing £118 profit (based on ingredient costs only). Naturally this is the most profitable way to sell ice cream and suitable if you have a van and live near the coast or a beauty spot. Larger quantities such a litre sized tub will command less direct profit, but it's still a great business, making you and your customers happy. Remember, selling a premium product requires a premium price, so don't sell yourself cheap! Information for starting an ice cream business can be found here **www.dairyscience.info/index. php/ice-cream/218-ice-cream-startup.html** .

In addition to everyday catering equipment, you will need specialised equipment, and storage. Equipment can be viewed and bought at **www.rsshereford.co.uk**, who run demonstration days.

Yoghurt is made by fermenting milk with a lactobacillus culture instead of rennet. Full-cream cow or sheep milk produces thick yoghurt, semi-skimmed a thinner product, and to add to the varieties, you could offer plain, fruit, or even yoghurt with honey added. You can use raw goat milk to make yoghurt also, but it's a little different to cow milk, so do a bit more research. Find out more and see some products here
https://gnltd.co.uk/collections/cheese-yogurt-making-1

Equipment starts around £3,000 for a 140 pot electric yoghurt maker, and the business is growing with movement towards artisan, natural brands or thicker Greek-style yoghurts. If you have access to your own raw ingredients this could be an on-farm business venture worth considering. A number of providers offer courses, including many agricultural colleges, such as Reaseheath in Cheshire **https:// reaseheathfoodcentre.com/yoghurt-manufacture/** .

Jams, preserves & chutneys

A favourite smallholding or home-based diversification project that keeps coming up for discussion on business courses I have organised, or at food fairs and markets I've attended, is that of jams and chutneys. Now, I like jam as much as the next person, but I'm going to put my head up above the parapet and look at the production of preserves as a business proposition. If you intend to produce and sell any kind of food product you need to be registered as a food producer with your local authority. You also need to have labels approved by Trading Standards with accurate weights displayed on labels, ingredients (ALL ingredients), allergens, and your name and address all on the label. You will need to demonstrate that your food production area is either permanent or temporary (in the case of a domestic kitchen), that you have a HACCP plan, separate hand-wash facilities, commercial storage etc.

You will have to really examine your costs, and take into account labour in the forms of harvesting, cooking, packaging and transporting time, ingredient production costs, utilities costings, packaging and labelling (new jars, not recycled), and any market stall fees. You will probably need public liability insurance, market stall insurance and product liability insurance.

If you are still serious about this, you will then have to examine who your ideal customer is, and what it is about your product that will appeal to them. What makes your chilli sauce or raspberry jam different from all the others out there? Then you have to produce this fabulous product at a price that will give you a profit – or else what is the point?

Pricing is so hard for new entrants into the food market. You must price your product either close enough to be comparable or at least at a price that you realistically think your customer will pay. If you work out the costs per jar, and price them to sell, giving you, for example, a generous profit of around 50p per unit, then you would need to sell 15,000 jars to realise a profit of £7,500. This means you'd have to sell 63 jars daily, for five days a week over 48 weeks in a year. If you are seriously looking about food production as a possible business, then trust me; there are less time-consuming and far more lucrative opportunities out there. However, if, like many older jam and chutney producers, you do it in order to socialise or chat about your produce and don't care about profit, by all means go ahead, but remember you'll still have to attend to the legal niceties.

Honey & beeswax

Beekeeping is one of those activities like poultry keeping where you can start small, covering your costs while you increase your confidence and skill, before gradually expanding into meaningful profitability without having to fund a huge capital outlay. One or two second-hand hives, a decent suit and a smoker will suffice for the first year or two whilst you learn the ropes, especially if you can join a decent local beekeeping group. The best way is to join the British Beekeepers Association (**www.bbka.org.uk**), where you will find a contact for your local group, and if you are lucky, a helpful and experienced mentor. They may also furnish you with a starter colony with a young laying queen. Many clubs have equipment for honey harvesting that can be borrowed or hired and experienced fellow beekeepers will talk you through the process. If you find yourself liking the hobby, then you can add to your own equipment, and start to think about selling your surplus.

You don't need a lot of land; in fact, many beekeepers keep a hive or two in their own small gardens or on local farmland, where the bees pollinate a whole range of crops. A square metre is sufficient for one hive and a small apiary of two or three hives will happily forage up to three miles from the hive to collect pollen and nectar. If you have to buy a new colony in the form of a "nuc", which comprises a young laying queen and five frames of bees and brood, you can expect to pay between £100 and £150. As you gain experience, you may be able to collect a swarm of bees to fill an empty hive and save yourself some expense.

As your colony numbers expand, you may be able to site more colonies in the gardens or orchards belonging to friends who are sympathetic to supporting honeybee numbers, but who do not wish to have the bother of looking after these important creatures. A site with a colony can expect a marked increase in pollination of fruit and vegetables, especially if the site is sheltered from cold winds and has a good variety of trees, shrubs or flowers.

Honeybees are pretty docile and respond well to gentle, confident handling, and it is only in thundery weather that they appear to become agitated. On the rare occasion that you receive a sting, scrape it off, take an anti-histamine tablet and put it down to experience. Checking the hives weekly takes a few minutes, to ensure the bees have enough room and that supers (the shallow box of frames where honey is stored) are not full and capped. A good summer could mean a harvest of around 60lbs of honey, but remember, you are at the mercy of the weather. A poor summer means the bees are confined inside the hive, eating the honey they have stored. In late summer, the harvest is removed, honey extracted from the frames, which are then replaced into the supers for the bees to clean and hopefully replace with new honey, and a varroa treatment added. A few weeks later, you'll need to check the hives to ensure the bees have enough honey to see them through winter and secure them against mice and greedy badgers.

Honey can be sold as liquid honey in jars, creamed honey or cut-comb honey, which commands a good price. There is a steady demand locally for honey, and an efficient beekeeper could own and manage 20-30 hives, kept over a few sites.

With a pound jar fetching around £6, and a small tub of cut-comb fetching around £10, there is a lucrative business to be made. Moving hives or nucs needs a little thought. Wait until the bees are inside at dusk, fit an entrance reducer or block or wad of sponge rubber, plug all holes and securely strap the hive or nuc inside your vehicle. Keep the temperature in the vehicle as cool as possible, drive smoothly, and when you arrive at your destination, take the hive carefully out, place in position and leave for half an hour before donning your suit and removing all the straps and wadding. The bees will reset their internal navigation over the next hour or so and be quite happy to explore their new home.

Beeswax is a secondary product produced by the bees. All the wax cappings of the honey in the supers, and any brace comb made by the bees to fill gaps between frames, can be collected by the clever beekeeper to either melt and reuse to make his own foundation sheets, or can be turned into wax blocks, candles or turned into cosmetics or wood polish. Selling at a minimum of £7 per pound, raw wax is much in demand, if you take the trouble to collect it.

As your colonies begin to outgrow your capacity, you may want to sell nucs of bees or starter colonies yourself as a little sideline. There are many tutorials of how to make nucs on the internet, and assembling these on winter days whilst you look forward to reaping the reward in the spring is time well spent.

Mead, Wines & Liqueurs

Discussing honey always makes me think of mead, that traditional and ancient alcoholic drink made from fermented honey. We know that mead was drunk in the Middle Ages, and even in biblical times, but there is now evidence to show that Neolithic man also enjoyed a form of mead. Some mead can be thick and incredibly sweet, and others dry and delicate like a fine sherry. A good many smallholders and country folk make mead, and many other alcoholic drinks, and some have turned this into a profitable business. The Queen of Denmark regularly orders cases of mead from a friend of mine, who produces a delicate, floral mead that is like drinking liquid sunshine. Whilst you are unlikely to enjoy such patronage, it may be a worthwhile product to add to your product range.

You can start small, with a range of normal kitchen equipment and winemaking covered buckets, and once you have perfected your product, expand to whatever size you feel you can comfortably supply. Remember to keep businesslike records and accounts, and work out your costings. If you enjoy filling your shed, garage or barn with bubbling buckets and gurgling airlocks, then adding some country wines may also be right up your street. I particularly enjoyed dandelion wine, dandelion beer and elderflower champagne, and all were ridiculously easy to make (and enjoy). It was this natural ability to make alcohol from fruit and flowers that led me to making cider, but I'll discuss that in another chapter.

Winemaking equipment and a vast array of bottles can be sourced easily and cheaply online. Get hold of a couple of well tried recipes and some wine yeast and give it a go. The hard part of the process is giving your finished product enough time to mature. A well-made fruit wine or mead can take up to a year to mature.

Artisan wine makers are on the increase in the UK as the climate is warming up and British palates have grown up since the 1970's when a bottle of *Blue Nun* was considered daring. The UK wine industry is growing at a tremendous rate with around 133 wineries covering around 2000 hectares, with around 503 vineyards. The most Northernly commercial vineyard is in Yorkshire, with most of the production centred in the southern counties and as far West as

Wales and Cornwall. Chardonnay (23%), Pinot Noir (22%), Bacchus (8%) and Pinot Meunier are the most commonly grown grape varieties, producing an average of 5.2m bottles of wine annually. The most successful and profitable wines are white sparkling Champagne type wines, and in May 2017, wine from a Norfolk vineyard was named as "the best white wine in the world" at the Decanter World Wine Awards (Winbirri Vineyards' Bacchus 2015).

UK wine production is one of the fastest growing agricultural products, and set to rise to around 10m bottles by 2020, with the acreage devoted to vineyards rising by 135% in the last 10 years. Vineyards can remain productive for twenty five to thirty years, but do not have full cropping potential till they are around four years old, and sparkling wine has to mature for two to three years, and this must be taken into account when long-term planning. There is a massive capital investment required for the sourcing and planting of vines, buildings construction, equipment, and expertise, and marketing. South facing slopes, the "right" soil and altitude less than 80m are required for optimum growing conditions. For details of UK wine regulations please see
https://www.food.gov.uk/business-industry/ winestandards
and excise details can be found at
https://www.gov.uk/government/publications/excise- notice-163-wine-production/excise-notice-163-wine- production.
Looking at the economics reveals that consumers will rarely pay over £10 per bottle of still wine, unless this is for a top class renowned product, and so UK producers are looking to maximise profit by selling direct to their customers (to achieve £10), rather than to wholesale to outlets and supermarkets. Producers have to pay VAT at 20%, plus duty and, if they sell via a wine merchant a margin of around 30%. The situation for sparkling wine is brighter, with retail prices commanding

£17- £27 per bottle, allowing for sufficient profit to pay for production costs.

An article in Horticulture Week in October 2016 suggested that Brexit could prove to be an excellent opportunity for UK wine producers, by allowing the government to revoke the "British" designation from products, as in the past the reputation of British wines has been fragile **http://www.hortweek.com/english-wine-producers-aim-boost-brexit/fresh-produce/article/1411821**.

Of course, many producers may decide to grow grapes and sell these on to existing winemakers and reduce their outlay and risk.

There has to be a catch of course, and the fly in the ointment is involvement with HMRC. While this may appear intimidating, there is a lot of guidance available on **www.gov.uk/guidance/wine-duty**. It's not as daunting as you think, and it's free to register. You will also have to read and adhere to the Excise Notice 163 monthly returns requirements, but bear in mind that you won't be the first person to walk down this path, and you certainly won't be the last! If you think you have a good product, have worked out your profit margin and are ready to present it to the thirsty world, then go for it. There are specialist consultants out there who can (for a price) help you to set up the necessary accounting and management systems required to comply with the HMRC rules.

Mead and fruit wines are taxed under the category, "made wines". This covers any alcoholic drink that isn't beer, cider, grape wine or spirits.

Liqueurs are a different animal altogether. If you make a liqueur by adding fruit or another flavouring to ready-made alcohol (ethanol), and intend to sell it, you MUST have a licence from HMRC as a compounder. You can find the required form (L5) here **www.gov.uk/government/publications/excise-application-for-an-excise-trade-licence-l5**. In addition you'll need to supply a list of the premises and plant you intend to use. HMRC cannot refuse permission provided the application is made correctly.

If you grow your own fruit this is an excellent way to add value to that fruit. Selling raw fruit will bring in a meagre profit and turning the fruit into pies or jams slightly more, but alcohol is far more profitable, even when taking into account the cost of the ethanol. Vodka is an excellent base spirit for fruit infusions or liqueurs, and some kitchen experimentation is fun and easy. Cherries, raspberries or sloes (blackthorn berries) can be added to vodka with the addition of some sugar, and after a few weeks drained out and stored in a cupboard for a few months to mature. Ensure your presentation is professional and slick. You'll have to compete with some established brands, but artisan gins, vodkas and now liqueurs are regaining popularity with a younger generation. The festive season is the main surge in the market, so plan your production to have everything in place for a big sales push starting at the beginning of December. Ethanol suppliers such as Alcohols Ltd in Birmingham and Haymankimia in Essex will point you in the right direction if you need any advice.

Beer and ale

The resurgence in popularity of small scale breweries and local ales offers an opportunity for farm diversification that many younger entrants have taken up. Naturally, you need to know a good beer when you taste it, but there are many courses out there to hone your skills. A microbrewery can be defined as an independent brewery making a relatively small amount of beer. They tend to focus on quality, flavour and technique. The work can be tedious and labour intensive, with a lot of cleaning. You'll have to contact HMRC for duty purposes and your local Environmental Health Officer to register as a food producer; Trading Standards will want input on labelling and you will also have to register on the Alcohol Wholesaler Registration Scheme **https://www.gov.uk/guidance/alcohol-wholesaler-registration-scheme-awrs-apply-to-register**

The good news is that now small scale beer-makers (producing up to 5000hl or around 880,000 pints) can enjoy 50% duty relief, with a tapering scale thereafter (Small Breweries Relief Scheme). More information available at **www.gov.uk**. Look for Excise Notice 226. Around 60% of the cost of beer making goes to excise duty, so this is not to be sniffed at.

As the process to make beer is relatively quick, prospective beer makers need a solid business plan and need to realise that marketing and selling are going to take up the majority of their time. There is a lot of competition out there and you will need to experiment with recipes to create something special and innovative marketing to ensure you reach the right customers. Whereas a home brewer will naturally go for a good 5% ABV beer, the market is looking for hoppy session ales (beers you will drink a few of) at a lower ABV of around 3.7- 4.5%. Checking out the free houses in your area will give you an idea of possible clients, but remember that pubs are in decline in the UK, with many going out of business. The market to focus on now would be the take home firkin or pin, excellent for home use, parties, events, weddings and festivals.

If you have suitable buildings, and these need not be huge when starting out, and a good supply of water, then this may be worth considering. A starter kit which can produce around 400 litres of beer at a time can be purchased for around

£10,000, whilst larger, more commercial set-ups can cost easily £40,000 second hand. You could cut costs by growing your own wheat or barley and hops and recycle most of the spent grain and yeast remains into animal feed and, by clever use of reed beds, allow water to be recycled back to the land. Just remember if you are planning to hit the large beer drinking population that are allergic to wheat, gluten free does not always mean wheat free. You need to mention any allergens on your packaging and remember that if you sell beer to pubs, pipes may be contaminated when swapping barrels around.

Meat and Meat Products

Meat and meat products are some of the highest earners for smallholders and rural businesses in the UK. Thankfully, the UK enjoys a highly regulated and traceable reputation, and the risks of spreading contagious illnesses such as bovine TB, foot and mouth disease and mad cow disease (variant Creutzfeldt-Jakob or vCJD) is rare. In fact, there have been no new incidences of vCJD since 2016. Salmonella infection is a common bacterial disease that can live in the intestines of both animals and humans, with humans being infected through contaminated food or water. Salmonella bacteria are most often found in raw meat, undercooked poultry, eggs and unpasteurised milk.

Two areas of concern to note are the methods of slaughter itself, and also the sadly, too frequent incidents of fraudulent labelling, where a food label may state that the meat contained therein is of one species, when in fact it is found to be contaminated with traces or even wholly another species. In 2017 the FSA (Food Standards Agency) found that in 665 samples, 145 were in fact partly or completely made up of unspecified meat. Processed meat (mince, sausages or curries) were the most commonly mis-labelled products.

You can slaughter and butcher animals on your own farm or property, if they are for your own or your family's consumption, and not for sale, and the details are here **www.food.gov.uk/safety-hygiene/home-slaughter-of-livestock**. There is also a "how to" section in the appendix of this book, detailing how to kill and prepare a chicken for your own consumption. If, as a smallholder you wish to slaughter and process your animals for meat to be sold, you will have to register as a food business, and the rules for slaughter and butchering are stringent. Read about the legal requirements here **www.food.gov.uk/business-guidanceindustry-specific-advice/meat-premises-and-slaughter**.

You may also wish to undertake some specific training, which can be found here **www.foodtraining.org.uk**

You'll have to consider that planning permission may be required, as although slaughter, cutting and packaging may be ancillary to your main business of smallholding or stock rearing, you may cause issues such as noise, smell, extra traffic movement and waste disposal. Discuss your plans with Environmental Health, Trading Standards, Finance (business rates may be imposed) and Planning, as change of use from agriculture to diversification into food production may be required. The discharge of sewage or other effluents requires contacting the Environment Agency, and completion of the form B6 (application for an environmental permit to discharge waste water) **https://www.gov.uk/government/publications/application-for-an-environmental-permit-part-b6-new-bespoke-water-discharge-activity-and-groundwater-point-source-activity**

Every local authority appears to deal differently with each individual application, and advice from an agricultural business surveyor or consultancy is best taken at the very

131

start of a project such as this.

Of course, you will be factoring in all these additional compliance costs, as well as waste disposal, vet's fees, packaging equipment & sundries, as well as feed, bedding, housing etc. Additional costs can be somewhat offset by growing your own animal feed and bedding, and if you can source the by-products of the cider and beer making industries to supplement feed, then this too may reduce the costs of keeping animals for meat. Food and drink businesses that supply by-products as animal feed must also comply with the EC Food Hygiene Regulation 183/2005 and Food Safety & Hygiene (England) Regulations 2013 (and their Scottish and Irish equivalent). In a nutshell, this means that to supply a pig farmer with your spent pomace as feed, you have to register with the council, produce a HACCP plan to show you have addressed the safety of the feed, after which you're given a registration number and possible inspection. Pomace, the remains of the apple pulp left over from juice or cider making, is full of sugar and protein. It must be fed fresh, and therefore stored properly. Pigs, sheep and cattle all enjoy some mixed in with their bland feed. The spent grains left over from brewing are also full of sugar, malt and protein and are similarly enjoyed by animals including poultry, as a supplement.

If you have decided that you are happy to undertake the paperwork and registration, then examine your market and your pricing. Your customers are the ones prepared to pay a little more for local, traditionally produced superior meat and meat products. Selling to local restaurants may make you a good name, but it's selling direct to the end consumer where you will make the most profit. Plain meat joints always sell for less than meat products that you have added value to, by turning them into sausages, salami or a stuffed rolled shoulder. Charcuterie is incredibly popular, as is artisan smoked dry-cure bacon. Do your homework, and try to add value wherever possible. Some pig producers I know actually avoid jointing, and process their whole animal into sausages as they simply make so much more money this way.

Remember to broadcast the fact that British farm welfare standards are amongst the best in the world. Whether you sell from an online shop, farmers market or from the farm itself, remember you are selling a quality product. Photographs of happy animals enjoying themselves in grassy pastures are much more appealing to the customer than the other reality of factory-farmed animals that never see the light of day. Embrace the idea of pork crackling, hog-roasts and Sunday lamb – the customer will love you for reminding them of traditional events, and pay a decent price for it too.

Starting a Smokery

Sausages and bacon are the meat products that most customers associate with smallholders, but with the public now being more cosmopolitan in their tastes and desires, pancetta, charcuterie and a variety of smoked foods are in great demand. My mother used to adore smoked salmon, and indeed the supermarkets are full of it, but smoked trout, sea-fish, even smoked scallops and eels are now regularly seen at artisan food markets. The range of smoked cheeses and garlic heads will make your mouth water, and fill the canny food producer's pockets.

There are two methods of smoking: hot, over a bed of charcoal or woodchips to slowly cook and flavour the food, or cold, where an unheated chamber is pumped full of smoke for between 12 and 48 hours. Fruitwood, oak or vine prunings seem to be the most popular at the moment, and all add a delicate taste to the food. Small smokers can be fabricated locally by an expert in stainless steel or bought over the internet, and courses are springing up all over the UK, from London, **www.londonsmokeandcure.co.uk/ smoke-school**, to Wales, **https://welshsmokery.co.uk/ workshops/** and of course in the North and Scotland. There is a wealth of information on the internet and YouTube on how to smoke, how to make a smoker, and the properties of different fuels used. My favourite is back-bacon rollups and scallops on skewers, hot smoked over apple wood chippings with a nice garlic mayo dip.

Nuts and Seeds

Nuts and seeds are enjoyed all over the UK, and not just by the health food or vegetarian market. They are increasingly sought after as snacks, cooking ingredients, and as a condiment to exotic recipes. Many of these can easily be grown within the UK, either as a hedgerow crop or as a stand-alone nut orchard or *plat*, as it was traditionally called.

Hazel, cobnuts, sweet chestnuts and with the increase of temperatures in the UK, even walnuts are grown as commercial crops in the UK. It may be possible to grow almonds in sheltered areas, but possibly never as a commercial venture. Christmas is a lucrative market, but when processed, into nut spreads, breakfast mueslis, and small packs for snacking, the time for sales can be extended to year-round. Marron glacé, or candied sweet chestnuts, were previously enjoyed in France or Spain, but many delicatessens in the UK now stock them, and pickled walnuts are a delight with good strong cheese and port. For younger consumers, chocolate or yoghurt coated nuts, honey roasted nuts and chilli nuts are becoming more popular, and offer many varieties for the producer to add value to an easy to grow product.

Hazelnuts grow wild all over the UK, with cultivated varieties mainly found in the southern counties of England, but this appears to be more by tradition than because of climate. They are tolerant of shade, and start cropping in their third year, from September to October. In full production at eight years old, a hectare can produce 3.5 tonnes, and a mix of varieties will ensure good pollination and reliability of production. The varieties Gunslebert, Butler and the "Kentish Cob" are readily available and good producers. Netting is necessary to protect the crop from squirrels.

Walnuts are uncommon in the UK, but can be grown in large, sheltered areas. They will produce a good harvest in around seven years and here in South West France we have our own walnut trees at our house. The nuts will drop themselves when ripe and we enjoy them throughout the winter, although neighbours do have their walnuts milled into oil. My one concern with them is that they seem to be very shallow rooted, and the summer storms that we have bring a lot down every year. Thankfully, ours are not planted too close to any buildings. You must plant them fairly far from other species of trees, as they release a toxin from their roots to inhibit competing vegetation. We favour the variety *franc*, but in the UK *Fernor* or *Lara* are good. Only in the far south of the UK will you achieve fully formed, ripe nuts, but they are excellent pickled when young.

Sweet chestnuts are large trees and like sandy, light soils. They grow quickly and are excellent for coppicing for firewood or for furniture. Good varieties are *Belle epin* or *Marigoule*. They are a favourite stuffing for wild boar (sanglier), and for many sausages from both wild boar and domestic pigs.

Add to this the proliferation of Asian style seed-mixes, snack bars, and seeds for adding to bread mixes, cakes and biscuits or for cookery purposes, and the growing of sunflower, fennel, caraway, poppy, pumpkin and other seeds can offer a discerning smallholder or niche food producer a range of products. Millet can be grown in warmer areas of the UK and is a useful snack or can be used as bird feed. As it is gluten-free it is being more widely produced and introduced into food products.

Seaweed

Seaweed has been collected and used within the UK as both a foodstuff and a soil improver for centuries. It was only in 2013 when wild seaweed harvest was estimated at around 2000-3000 dry tonnes, and in fact there are now a few small and one large commercial seaweed farm in the seas around the UK.

Sea vegetables, including laverbread, carrageen and dulce, are used as a food and condiment, mainly in the Asian food market, although the health food market is growing. As a fast-growing, robust, sustainable and nutritious crop, it has been estimated that a potential harvest of 24 tonnes per hectare annually is possible. The Scarborough based SeaGrown farm was founded in 2018, and is a 25 hectare offshore farm, the largest offshore seaweed farm located in open sea, as opposed to the smaller farms located at inlets and sea lochs. Still in its infancy, the farm aims to be able to supply not only the food industry, but also cosmetics, pharmaceuticals, fertilizers and animal feed manufacturers. The market is a huge one and SeaGrown are trying to balance the ability to expand the farm against the risk of the location, exposed to the might of the North Sea. There are other small seaweed farms, mainly processing kelp for industrial uses in the West coast of Scotland. This is an emergent sector in the UK, but certainly one worth keeping an eye on in future. For smallholders and crofters located in coastal areas there may be future opportunities within this sector if the trend catches the public imagination.

Polytunnels

Wherever you are located in the UK, a polytunnel will lengthen your growing season and allow you to grow a variety of crops that you may struggle to produce in open land. We are not just talking about exotics such as tomatoes and chillies here, but traditional soft fruits such as strawberries and raspberries, and crops such as salads, cut flowers and early vegetables.

In Scotland, the soft fruit industry has revolutionised the production of strawberries and raspberries extending their season by many weeks, and reaping the benefits of growing under plastic. They can control and stagger production to avoid gluts, reduce disease and control pollination.

With the resurgence in demand for local products, canny producers near to the cities located in the midlands are producing salad crops, tomatoes and exotic herbs for the hospitality sector. In the southern counties, out-of-season French beans, mini-vegetables, and exotics such as wasabi are readily snapped up by a voracious demand from London.

Investing in a polytunnel offers many opportunities away from straight crop growing too. Purpose-built tunnels can be used in late winter as lambing shed, and then once the season is finished, returned to protected fruit or vegetable production, temporary dry storage for hay or other crops, or even as a classroom for teaching smallholding courses! I strung up a washing line inside mine to allow drying of clothes in inclement weather.

The market for forced fruit, salads, chillies and vegetables is a growing one, and aside from the normal markets of supermarkets, farmers markets, artisan shops and direct sales for good quality produce, large quantities of slightly imperfect fruit can be sold to jam makers, yoghurt and ice cream makers, soft drink producers and country wine producers.

The siting and erection of polytunnels can be subject to planning restrictions, so check your local planning rules. There are different rules depending on the size of the polytunnel, whether it is temporary or a permanent structure, and on the size of your land. Generally, if the proposed tunnel is less than 3m tall, for domestic use and takes up less than 50% of the space in your garden you do not require planning permission. All polytunnels intended for commercial use require planning permission, as do all tunnels over 3m tall (commercial use or not). The question of whether polytunnels require permission is not found in legislation, but in case law tests, all relating to size, permanence and physical attachment.

For any proposed development (including polytunnels), the size of an agricultural holding is important. If five hectares (12.35 acres) or more, then there are certain permitted development rights under the Town and Country Planning (General Permitted Development) Order 2015. Part 6 relates to agricultural and forestry development and allows for the erection of a building (including a polytunnel) which is reasonably necessary for agricultural purposes within that unit. Therefore, a single polytunnel would only require prior notification. Multiple polytunnels are restricted, however, and you are advised to seek clarification locally.

Issues that arise when planning applications for commercial ranges of polytunnels are submitted include economic need and impact, landscape and visual impact, residential amenity, transport and roads, water, biodiversity, rights of way, and archaeology.

Prices for domestic sized tunnels start from £200, with larger commercial tunnels from £2000. Aside from the initial investment in a tunnel, you may, depending on your intended use, require internal automated watering, waste water reclamation, table-top staging or plant support. Then, if producing soft fruit or salads, you'll need to think of food prep areas, refrigerated storage and packaging areas.

Edible Flowers

The UK cut flower market has had to evolve, under the relentless pressure of cheap Dutch imports, and now has created and supplies a growing demand for woody ornamentals, wild flowers and flower varieties that even just twenty years ago, would have never been seen in high street florists. The shop-local ethos, and a change in taste, has reached the flower market and there is a demand for quality local blooms and a large variety of floristry foliage. Whilst the growing of eucalyptus, winter blossoms such as jasmine, sweet box and variegated evergreens can provide local florists with much needed out-of-season greenery, some smallholders are also starting to supply the growing market for edible flowers.

Restaurants, cafes, high class food stores are increasingly stocking a variety of edible flowers such as borage, herbs, onion flowers, and small delicate violets and primroses for cake decoration. There is a huge market online and growers who can supply quick delivery in protected packaging within the UK will find a demand for both special occasions and routine orders from high-class restaurateurs.

If you are located in an area that can support fruit and vegetable production, and are happy to invest in a very hands-on product, then consider cultivating saffron. The saffron crocus (Crocus sativus) blooms in autumn, and used to be widely cultivated in the UK in the middle-ages. The plants are delicate, and planting, harvesting and processing require delicate handling. It is the stigmas in the flower that are carefully picked and dried, and you'll need a lot of bulbs for meaningful production and they are an ideal permanent catch-crop for autumn. An ideal crop for protected production, inside well ventilated polytunnels with a bed of light, silty soil, your saffron would be much in demand. With attractive packaging, this premium product could fetch £150 for 2g of saffron. Whilst this sounds fabulous, understand that dried saffron is very light, and a single bulb produces just three stigmas (strands of saffron).

Registering as a Food Producer in the UK

To carry out any kind of food business, whether it be selling, cooking, storing, handling or distributing food, you are required to register this business with your local district or county council at least 28 days before starting the business. All premises that you use to carry out this business must be registered, even if you are home-based or in a mobile stall or van. Registration is free and cannot be refused, although most local authorities will 'advise' you if they feel your premises or practices need updating or are substandard in any way. You can find out more information here **www.food. gov.uk/business-guidance/register-a-food-business**. The exception would be food businesses that make, prepare or handle meat, fish, egg or dairy products for supply to other businesses (not direct to the end consumer), who may require approval by the local authority, not registration.

I have personally found that having a chat with my Environmental Health Officer before starting any new business means we start on a level footing, and I have found them to be incredibly helpful. In fact, if it hadn't been for the chats I had with our EHO in Cornwall, I would have never started my cider business! I was so put off by the paperwork, regulations and frankly, found it all a bit overwhelming.

My EHO explained the process, the forms and helped me complete them in a short space of time, and I never looked back.

CASE STUDY –
Polmarkyn Dairy

Katie Wood
Brook Barn Farm
Cornwall
www.polmarkyndairy.co.uk
https://www.facebook.com/katiesgoats/

Katie Wood and her partner Glyn Thomas bought their 18-acre farm in early 2016, so their business is a fairly new venture. Glyn is a mechanic, but Katie had previous experience as a dairy maid at a cheese farm in Gloucestershire. Brook Barn Farm is a small cottage with some outbuildings, surrounded by typical small Cornish paddocks with medium to poor grazing.

Katie and Glyn run a small herd of around 50 pedigree goats, and have transformed existing farm buildings into a dairy, winter housing and space for their businesses to expand. They have invested their own money into the business. The goats are a mix of British Alpine, British Toggenburg, Golden Guernsey and British Saanen goats. The working day normally starts at 4am with milking, but in kidding season hours can be erratic and through the night.

Polmarkyn won gold at the 2017 Cornish Cheese and Dairy Awards for her goats milk. Katie uses social media and word of mouth to sell her products from the farm, markets and via wholesalers. She supplies milk and cheese to a London restaurant and milk and other restaurants in Cornwall, so the future is looking very good!

Since 2019 Katie has increased the product range, and now produces goat meat and sausages and goats milk soap. The majority of income is from fresh raw goats milk, yoghurt and goats cheese. As producing milk, yoghurt and cheese from raw milk is a little unusual, Katie has had an interesting time convincing the local council of the safety of the product.

Quote – "If you have a dream, go for it! We make enough to cover bills, but we are here all the time and so have no social life, which suits us. The biggest pain we had has been with the council, as we wanted to sell raw milk and make cheese from raw milk."

Chapter 6
Money Growing on Trees

This whole chapter is all about orchards and orchard products, which are undervalued as an asset to smallholdings and gardens all over the UK. An orchard, or even a single tree has the potential to produce a successful crop for anyone who wishes to fill their larder or freezer with produce, to supplement their livestock feed and to make juice or cider. But they can produce a really good profit for a smallholder or householder with a large garden. Quality apples can be sold for many months to artisan shops, sold at farmers markets and direct to the customer, looking for local produce. Windfalls and apple and pear pomace can be used to supplement animal feed, and a myriad of juices, ciders, perry and other drinks can also be produced from your orchard. They are easy to grow, demand very little maintenance, and can be used to double or even triple-crop, with fruit growing in the trees, sheep or chickens foraging underneath and bees housed along the margins.

There is the timeless passage of the seasons, marking family occasions from christenings to weddings, and enjoying the reward of eating a ripe, sun-warmed apple that you have grown and nurtured yourself. From blossom time through to harvest, the orchard adds beauty to any setting, and offers a place to escape to; a refuge from the noise and clamour of the house or office, where you can enjoy the drowsy buzzing of the honeybees in the blossom and marvel at the swelling and colouring of the fruits. Orchards are made to make memories, whether they are taking your youngster to hospital after that first fall out of a tree, or the clearing up after that memorable wassail celebration. You may even commemorate the passing of a loved one by planting a special tree. As the branches bend under the weight of ripe apples with their honeyed sweetness, it will certainly add to your delight when you realise that you are almost watching money grow on trees.

Apples are incredibly versatile. They come in three main types and thousands of varieties. There are dessert apples (eaters), culinary apples (cookers), and cider apples. The wild cards, crab apples and wildlings, can be used for jams, chutneys or added to juice or cider. There are commercial varieties grown by the million for their sweetness, pest and disease resistance and keeping properties, and there are old-fashioned heritage varieties, sometimes homely to the eye, but with an unmatched flavour, which may only be found in one or two orchards in out-of-the-way gardens or old orchards.

By focussing on your customers, your location and the local competition, you could easily base your marketing on spotlighting local varieties and sell these for up to five months of the year. Supermarkets are only interested in huge quantities and offer a remarkably low price to apple growers in the UK, so sell direct to the customer, who wants local, traditional delicious apples that you just cannot source at large shops. Consumers can be teased, coaxed, and won-over at apple days, tasting sessions at the farm or at farmers markets. They will be captivated by your colourful website with fabulous photos of the orchard in blossom with spring sunlight dappling the ground. A short video of the honeybees in their painted hives in the orchard will transport them on-site. Information on the varieties grown, presented in short bursts will have them drooling to taste Queenie's or Beauty of Bath, have them smile at names such as Slack Ma Girdle and Bottlestopper, and itching to learn more about the story of The Bloody Ploughman, or why an apple was called Peasgood Nonsuch (Mrs Peasgood, from Lincolnshire had an apple tree with apples of surpassing flavour that "nonesuch" could match them).

There are literally thousands of varieties, so you'll need to decide early on what you want to plant. My advice? Well, if you fancy eating apples from August till December, then choose one (or more) early, mid and late variety. There are many easy, disease-resistant varieties with great taste, but for early cropping, I like Katy and Discovery, for mid-season, Cox's Orange Pippin and Spartan, and for late season Orleans Reinette and Cornish Gilliflower. Now these are just a few suggestions, but you have a whole world of apples to choose from.

Want to plant a cooking apple? Please consider all varieties and don't just choose a Bramley. They have a great taste, yes, but they are notorious for scab and canker, especially in the damper areas of western Britain. There are so many other varieties, such as Scotch Bridget, Annie Elizabeth, and the triple purpose Orleans Reinette. Remember, the clever smallholder wants to plant trees that are as trouble-free as possible.

Dessert apples are great to sell to customers wanting lunchbox fruit, and small quantities of fruit for the fruit bowl, but they will buy in small quantities, so you may be left with rather a lot of unsold apples, which, especially for the early varieties, don't store well. So if you cannot sell your whole crop, then juice it! Fresh juice will keep in the fridge for a maximum of three days. Pasteurising it will extend the shelf life for at least a year. If you think you may be bored with juice, then turn it into cider.

Cider can be made from virtually any apples, and in south-eastern England it is mainly dessert apples that are used. Traditionally in the West country and the midlands specific cider varieties are grown and cider was mainly produced from these. Tastes are changing and modern cider makers incorporate a mix of dessert and cider fruit, and the trend is towards sweeter, sparkling cider; however, making your own cider, whatever apples you include, and whatever style you make, will give you a fabulous, local, artisanal product that could generate a large profit if you learn to make good cider.

So, if you fancy making some cider, you'd better add some specific cider varieties to that orchard you're planning. It's the balance of sugar, acid and tannins that determines which category of apples a variety falls into. Cider apples are either bittersweet or bittersharp, but they are also structurally different from dessert (sweet) or cooking apples (sharp). The cell structure is more robust and they can feel somewhat 'dry' to taste. They are usually incredibly unpleasant to eat raw, and I have fond memories as a tutor, teaching cider-making, when asking students to identify apples into their respective groups by tasting. The chosen bittersweet was Ashton Bitters, and it's the worst tasting apple I've ever grown, but makes incredible cider. I can only tell you they taste like chewing a really old, wet teabag, and in 100% of cases were spat into the tasting bucket. The juice and cider they create, however, is like drinking liquid sunshine, so this variety is well worth including in your orchard.

Crab apples and wildlings are only really good for pollination or for leaving the fruit for your orchard wildlife, unless you make some jelly or preserve from them. Apples are extremely promiscuous and will happily breed all sorts of strains, but never breed true to the parent tree. This is why,

147

when people ask if they can grow an apple tree from pips, I tell them yes, but they'll have to then use it as a rootstock and graft a known variety onto it.

Establishing an Orchard

If you have even a small garden you could plant an apple tree, and enjoy the blossom and fruit from it. The fortunate smallholder may already benefit from an established orchard, but if not, and you have at least a sixth of an acre, I urge you to consider planting one. From planting one year old maiden grafted trees to being able to harvest a half decent crop can take up to seven years, depending on the rootstock of the tree, the location, altitude, average rainfall and the quality and depth of your soil. In Cornwall, after a false start in the front garden of our smallholding, where the soil was shallow and shillety, I replanted the young trees in our small paddock in the rear of the land, where the soil was good quality and deep, and had the benefit of an established shelter belt to protect the orchard from the fierce south-westerly winds. The shelter belt was supplemented with some hazel plants to produce nuts for Christmas time, whilst also thickening the hedge.

Apart from very old traditional varieties which have been originally grown on their own roots, most modern varieties are clones of the parent, either grafted or budded onto the chosen rootstock. Grafting is probably easier for the beginner, and I have included a 'how to' section in the rear of this book if you fancy trying it yourself.

Rootstocks

The rootstock of the apple comprises the root ball with a short section of trunk or stem, which stands about six to nine inches proud of the soil. This is then topped with the scion, or variety of apple, which comprises the remainder of the trunk and the branches and leaves. The choice of rootstock will determine the vigour and size of the adult tree, and can also bestow some disease resistance to the tree itself.

The overall size of the tree at maturity is important to know as this will govern how many trees you will be able to plant in an area of ground, and will also affect how you deal with harvesting and pruning. The planting density also depends on the soil, climate and aspect of the site. The table below has suggested spacings based on average conditions. Be wary of trying to squeeze in more trees if you think you have near-perfect conditions, as your trees will respond to optimum conditions by growing larger (in height and spread) and faster. On the other hand, if you suffer from drought in summer, and poor soil, then opting for a larger rootstock will provide the trees with some extra vigour to cope with these trying conditions. In Dordogne, apples are difficult to succeed with, and my MM106 grafted trees have not flourished in our testing dry climate; perhaps, with hindsight, I'd have been better to choose M111 or M25 rootstocks.

In my orchard in Cornwall, my MM106 rootstocks produced lovely half-standard trees that were easy to prune and harvest by hand, without the necessity of ladders or machinery to reach branches. A quarter of an acre could support as many as 75 trees, which as you can see from the table amounts to an awful lot of apples! Half-standards start to branch at around 1-1.5 metres, so they are a good choice for smaller trees, which can allow grass cutting or harvesting around the base.

Full standards are normally grown on M25 rootstocks and these can grow into very large trees. Machinery can easily be driven under the canopy, but pruning needs some planning, and harvesting is usually by machine.

In the table below, I've listed the common UK rootstocks with their particular attributes. This will give you the information to be able to plan your own new orchard. Measure all spacings from stem to stem, and mark the position with a cane before you dig the holes. Start by measuring at least five metres from any existing hedges or trees, who will out-compete with your new trees. Remember that trees form a root system underground of a similar shape and spread of the canopy above ground. According to the table, this means a 10m x 10m plot can accommodate either one M25 tree or four MM106 trees, but this is a guide only. Another complicating factor is to check whether your chosen varieties are diploid or triploid. For these purposes you just need to know that triploid trees tend to be stronger and more vigorous growers, taking up more room. I like to keep all my early croppers together, then my mid season, then finally my lates. This allows for different varieties in each group to pollinate each other at the same time, and I get a good setting of fruit. Remember and make a reference plan of the orchard with the variety of each tree, so that at harvest time, you know what you are harvesting and for what purpose.

Table 1 Rootstock explanation

Apples rootstock	M27	M9	M26	MM106	MM111	M25
Ultimate height	1-2m	2-3m	2.9-3.5m	3.5-5.m	4.5-6m	6.5 - 9m
soil	Good, deep, fertile soil. Permanent stake. No competition.	Good, deep, fertile soil, permanent stake. No competition.	Good, deep, fertile soil. Stake for 5 years. Growing in grass will slow growth.	Can tolerate heavier soils & exposed conditions. Can be grown in grass. Remove stake after 5 years.	Tolerates most soils & conditions. Grows in grass. Remove stake after 5 years.	Most soils & conditions. Good pest/disease resistance. Grows in grass or hedge. Remove stake after 5 years.
spacing	5-6 ft 1.5-1.8m	5-6 ft 1.5-1.8m	10 ft 3m	12 ft 3.6m	22-25 ft 7-8m	25 -30 ft 7.6-9m
Years to fruiting	2-3 yrs	2-3 yrs	3-4 yrs	3-4 yrs	5-6 yrs	6-7 yrs
uses	Cordon, patio tree, Patio/pots	Cordon, step over, bush. Small garden.	Cordon, step over, espalier, bush. Med garden.	Espalier, fan, bush, half standard. Med-large garden, schools.	Standard. Community orchard, farm/traditional orchard. Replaces MM106 in challenging areas.	Standard. Farm/traditional orchard
Yield at 10 yrs	7kg	20kg	30kg	50kg+	90kg+	120kg+

Bare root trees are cheaper to buy than pot grown, and usually healthier, but maidens and two year old trees are fairly costly. After three years of buying in bare root trees I learned how to grow rootstocks and how to graft them. This saved me considerable sums of money and also allowed me to both teach this as a one day course, and to create and sell my own apple trees. See the guide to grafting apple trees in the appendices at the rear of this book.

Funding for Orchards

Years of austerity have depleted what little funding there was for planting new orchards, but there are a few avenues to explore. Much of the funding is for community or school orchards, but I have found a few places where farmers and land-owners can still access funding, although be aware in the current uncertain times we live in, this may change suddenly.

The People's Trust for Endangered Species has grant funding available, but you'll need to check the conditions, here
https://ptes.org/campaigns/traditional-orchard-project/orchard-grants/
The Rural Payments Agency and Natural England still offer funding under the Higher Tier Countryside Stewardship scheme. This is for the creation of traditional orchards, i.e. trees on M25 or M111 rootstocks. There is more information here
www.gov.uk/countryside-stewardship-grants/creation-of-traditional-orchards-be5

The Prince's Countryside Fund's Open Grants Scheme is currently being reviewed, but they have offered funding to improve the viability of farms and rural businesses all over the UK, and are keen to support projects that have a long-term positive impact.

www.princescountrysidefund.org.uk/grant-giving-
programme/grant-programme

If you live within Snowdonia National Park have a look at
this funding
https://www.snowdonia.gov.wales/looking-after/
woodlands/orchard-trees-grant

Again, in Wales, **The Sustainable Development Fund
(SDF)** is available in the Welsh part of the Wye Valley
AONB. It can be used to support innovative and sustainable
projects involving local communities within and adjacent
to the AONB. The grant is delivered by the Wye Valley
AONB Unit, on behalf of the Welsh Government. Private
individuals can apply for small grants for the purposes of
orchard planting or gap filling.
www.wyevalleyaonb.org.uk/caring-for-wye-valley-aonb/
grants/grants/

Pruning & Maintenance

If you have chosen varieties that are disease and pest
resistant, then your maintenance of the orchard should be
limited to pruning and harvesting. You may, even if you
undergraze the orchard with hens or sheep, need to top the
grass occasionally too.

Pruning the trees will give them the necessary structure
to perform at their best, and early removal of damaged or
diseased wood aids the health of the tree. Winter pruning
must be carried out when the tree is fully dormant. In the far
North of the UK, this is between December and March; in
the far south the window of opportunity is tighter, between
January and mid February.

Winter pruning can be as simple or as complicated as you
wish, and there are many tutorials on the internet. I try to

keep things simple and remove dead, diseased and damaged parts, and then I stand back and look at the shape. Anything sticking out to the top off to one side is pruned back to an outward facing bud, to try and coax the tree into growing into a wine-glass shape. Of course, some varieties are vagabonds and insist on growing with a drooping shape, almost like a weeping willow, in which case I just stick to dead, diseased and dying and leave the tree to it. If I have to remove any larger branches then I leave the wound bare. The experts all agree now that painting the cut surface actually does more harm than good. Summer pruning is the removal of any sappy growth or cutting back to just above fruit trusses, and aids formation of the following year's fruit buds. In standard or half-standard trees this is required very infrequently, and unless you have a vast amount of leaf canopy preventing fruits from receiving the sun, I'd be tempted not to bother. Winter pruning stimulates growth and controls congestion inside the canopy. Any branches reaching for the sky can be chopped to whatever you think the final height should be.

Intensive production employs a much more regimented approach, to force production and to ensure that harvesting equipment can freely pass between the rows. These intensive set-ups frequently employ sward eradication to reduce competition for nutrients. Remove all prunings and burn.

If you have the misfortune to have your orchard located in a frost pocket, then there are things you can do to try and lessen the problem. Firstly, cold air travels along the ground and can be diverted away from trees by the positioning of baffles in the form of low hedging, grown close to the ground. This can change the directional flow of the cold air and reduce the chance of frost slightly. A sharp frost or deep freeze for a few days can damage some of the blossom, and therefore reduce the cropping of your trees, but personally I've never been too badly affected by this. Apples, pears and even plums and cherries are quite hardy.

Finally, when the blossoms have been pollinated and fruit is set, you may be aware of the phenomena known as "June drop", which is when the tree sheds a few of the many tiny fruitlets. A truss of blossom is usually made up of four or five individual flowers, which all have the chance of becoming pollinated and becoming apples. Five apples in such close proximity is a big burden for a twig, so after the June drop, I like to move about my trees, removing any excess fruitlets and reducing the truss to two or three per twig. Obviously, I can't do this to every twig on every tree, but on younger trees it reduces the burden of weight on slimmer branches.

Undergrazing

Traditional orchards are natural pastures that can support more than just a crop of apples. The orchard can be undergrazed by chickens, ducks and lambs, who will keep the grass short, fertilizing the ground as they graze. Beware of allowing full grown sheep and goats into your orchard unless the trees are mature and full standards, or you will find the animals making a meal of the lower branches. Similarly, geese are known to strip off the bark of young trees. Pigs, of course, can be put for a short time into orchards after the harvest to recycle any windfalls, but must be removed before they start to dig up the orchard. Even Kune-Kune or Pot Belly Pigs are natural rooters and are best kept well away from such a precious resource.

If you have taken the time and expense to plant a new orchard, protect this with good staking and tree guards. Rabbits and deer are very partial to tasty young trees, especially in the winter months, and damage to young bark could severely affect the growth and even kill the trees.

Harvest

The most difficult period in the apple-grower's year is the harvest, not just because the work itself is hard, but also because it takes a great deal of organising and nature itself isn't necessarily all that co-operative. Organising the harvest will have started right back when you decided what varieties to plant because they all crop at different times, from August through until December.

Testing for ripeness is a priority, and there are a few signs to indicate when a fruit is ripe, including cutting it open to reveal the pips. If the pips are brown the apple is ripe; half brown, then leave for another week, and check again. The fruit should part from the twig easily. If you have to tug it, it's probably not ripe. Some ripe varieties also have a greasy texture to their skin. Strong autumn winds may produce windfalls, but these may not be ripe, so you could collect these and store in shallow boxes to allow the sugars to develop for a week or so.

Harvesting can be done by hand or machine, and will depend on the size of your orchard, labour costs and availability of appropriate machinery. If you're fortunate to live in one of the traditional orchard-growing areas, you may be able to hire a contractor to come and do the harvest for you. Apples destined for eating or for juicing must be picked from the tree, not from the ground. This prevents bruising and contamination from soil-borne pathogens and bacteria. The early apples tend not to store well, unless refrigerated, so ensure you have arranged collection for your trade buyers as soon as possible after harvest. Any windfalls, and all of the cider apples, and any unsold dessert fruit, are processed for cider, with the spent pomace being recycled into animal feed.

Although it sounds idyllic to be out in the orchard in the

autumn sunshine harvesting apples, it's more often than not conducted in wet weather, which turns quickly to mud. There are a myriad of wasps, hornets and slugs and it's heavy and tiring. If you are a small outfit, you may be picking on your own and that gets very lonely and demoralising. Keeping the ground under the trees as bare as possible and using plastic rakes to gather the fruit together helps. Stubborn apples can be shaken from the trees onto tarpaulins, instead of fiddling around with dangerous ladders. Use plastic fruit crates or rigid gardening sacks to avoid damaging the fruit during transportation. Try to avoid overloading. 25kg per crate or sack is the maximum for lifting safely.

We enlisted the help of volunteers to help us at harvest time, using ads placed on the HelpX website. The response came mainly from university students and older itinerant workers, looking for board, lodging, and either pocket-money or the chance to learn how to make cider. We had a caravan big enough for two with toilet, washing and cooking facilities. You need to assure yourself about insurance, health and safety considerations and, the law if you intend to employ staff.

Keep your picked apples and your windfalls separate, as windfalls must not be used in juice production because of the possibility of Patulin infection (see Juicing below).

If you sell cider apples to the trade, you may realise quite different pricing depending on your location and the demand in your area. Sadly, during the Covid pandemic, many large cider makers ended fruit contracts, and despite an increase in consumer demand for fresh fruit, issues with staffing, packaging and transportation have meant unpicked crops, a glut in fruit and costs escalating. Sadly, the apple grower has increased costs and problems whilst the price has dropped. Although this situation is thought to be temporary, it leaves many apple farmers facing the crunch, (if you'll excuse the pun).

Some of the early cider ferments very quickly as the temperatures in September and early October are still quite high, and this cider can be later be blended with the more tannic varieties produced by the later harvest of cider apples. Cider making for us in Cornwall carried on until the start of December, with fermentation continuing throughout winter, although we could be drinking our own early cider at Christmas. Here in France, apple harvests for dessert fruit are during August and September, and for cider fruit from October to December.

The top fruit growers in the UK are facing hard times. In 2019 the value of dessert fruit increased, but the price of cider apples fell, mainly due to a drop in demand from cider makers. This was the result of a huge increase of cider trees planted in the 1990s which had now reached peak production. The large cider makers, including Bulmers and Heineken, could not absorb the increased production and there was a glut on the market; prices fell and this led to many cider orchards being grubbed up. The average price of a tonne of cider apples in 2019 was around £90-£120. Then with the combined double-whammy of Brexit fears and Covid-19 restrictions, consumer demand resulted in a huge demand for fresh dessert apples and pears, which at such short notice could not be supplied from UK stocks. Pubs closed, social distancing and restrictions meant cider sales dropped, orders were cancelled, production stalled and now, the price of cider apples has dropped again. I would hesitate to plant a full cider orchard now, but the market for local, craft cider is still in its ascendancy, so I'd opt for planting a mixed orchard; some dessert and some cider trees, perhaps one or two pears, plums and some cherries. Dessert fruit has increased in value, with traditional varieties gaining in popularity, but planting apple trees means an enforced 6 year minimum wait till they are producing fruit, and who knows what the market trends will be at that time.

Milling & pressing

It's frequently said that cider is one of the most ancient alcoholic beverages on earth, but anyone who has tried to press a worthwhile quantity of apples without the aid of a mechanical press will confirm that this is incredibly hard work, and the lever-press wasn't documented until about 160BC.

Apples are substantial fruit, and have to be ground to a pulp in a mill before the resulting pulp can be squeezed to extract juice. So, straight away, you need two pieces of equipment. For small-scale production, a simple scratter mill could cost as little as £80 online. A more robust electric version could cost as much as £200-£300. A small, round table-top press can be home made, there are many plans online, but again, this is really for very small hobby producers. Jump in volume and you really require a water-driven hydropress, rack and cloth press or belt press and you can expect to pay upwards of £2000.

The juice yield will depend on many factors including the variety of apples, the efficiency of the press and the quality and age of your apples. A hydraulic jack fitted to your rack and cloth press will allow quicker extraction with less effort.

Juice

I only produced enough juice for our own small requirements, choosing not to begin commercial production for a few reasons. Firstly, Cornwall and Devon already had a few apple juice producers, and secondly the food hygiene rules were more complex than those pertaining to cider production, because unlike fermented cider, fruit juices are packed full of sugars, which bacteria love. However, top fruit and soft fruit juice and cordials are both profitable businesses for anyone also considering cider production, as you will already have to obtain roughly the same equipment.

Your EHO officer will explain all about the requirement for white rooms for juice production, bottling and storage, and may even email you an example HACCP plan with detailed procedures for you to employ and show due diligence, and that you have accounted for any possible source of contamination.

You will need to examine every step in the production process from before harvesting, when you remove any animals or poultry from the orchard six weeks prior to harvest, to thorough washing and inspection of fruit prior to milling. This means ensuring that all fruit is visually checked for quality, bird or insect damage, rodent contamination, before pressing. Glass bottles must be washed to remove all traces of glass or insect debris, before filling with juice, which must then be pasteurised efficiently.

Patulin is a mycotoxin produced by fungi that can grow on the surface of and inside apples, if it has entered via an open calyx (the bottom end of the apple, opposite the stalk). It is a worldwide problem and particularly common in unfermented apple-based products, such as juice and apple sauce. An increased incidence of Patulin infection has been proven where apples have been stored to ripen, as the softening fruit is more susceptible to the pathogen. Including sulphur dioxide preservative during the juicing process, and refrigeration, will reduce but not totally eliminate the pathogen. It's impossible to detect visually, and pasteurisation will not destroy it, and so to show due diligence, you are advised to have thorough record keeping, with frequent small samples sent for microbial analysis.

The profit margin is certainly lower than that of the same quantity of cider, and the risks somewhat higher. Because the fermentation process employed in producing cider creates both alcohol and carbon dioxide, which kill the mycotoxin, you may decide, like I did, that on balance juice was better produced on a small domestic scale for my own enjoyment, whilst cider was a highly lucrative commercial proposition.

Cider

After producing small amounts of cider for ourselves for around three years, we took advice from our very helpful EHO regarding the commercial cider production and the formalities relating to this. She made a site visit and we discussed integrating the changes required prior to officially starting, including a washing station, white room bottling, record keeping, and labelling requirements. I already had a contact at a food testing laboratory, and had undertaken Food Hygiene certification when we had set up as an Egg Producer.

Our aim was to make good craft cider from 100% local apples and sell it locally. At the start, John and I did the pressing, but as production doubled every year, we soon had some volunteers at harvest time to cope with the increasing volume of fruit, juice and waste. We had volunteers from all over the world coming to exchange their labour for food and lodging and learning how to make cider. It's a great idea, and we learned equally from people from a wide variety of backgrounds and cultures. We could never have afforded to take on seasonal staff, but volunteers helped us with some of the bigger jobs on our smallholding.

The cider section in any supermarket expands every year, but a close examination of the label on the rear of a bottle will reveal a lot about the production method, and about the cider contained therein. Many well-known brands will not list apple juice as their main ingredient. In fact, you may be shocked to see water, followed by sugar or glucose syrup as the main ingredient. Proper, REAL, artisan cider is made with 100% apple juice and, if cider is a product you want to make, then be ethical and stick to this and your customers and fan-base will love you. Your bank manager will love you too, because this is a really profitable business to be in, even small scale, like I did.

Complete form CP33, **www.gov.uk/government/publications/alcohol-duties-claim-for-exemption-from-registration-by-a-maker-of-cider-or-perry-for-sale-cp33** to become a duty-exempt producer and produce and sell up to 7,000 litres of cider without paying duty or becoming a registered alcohol wholesaler (although that quantity does include cider made for your own use, and the moment you pass 7,000 litres you have to pay duty on your entire output). This exemption has given many cidermakers the opportunity to start small, and then either perfect their product and expand, or keep the business small and artisanal, supplying a niche product locally. This latter is the approach I took. I wanted to be able to tell my customers what varieties were in each batch, where they came from, and how I made it, and to enjoy making my cider instead of having the business run me.

I used apples from around 40 cider and dessert trees, and at my busiest produced 4,000 litres annually. It was hard work, but I could easily make a good wage from it; and with a ready market locally I didn't even have to think about internet sales. I produced six ciders, which let me hit just about all markets in the area. I made still cider in medium and medium-dry either bottled or bag-in-box – 20L for pubs and 5L for take-home. I also made bottle-conditioned

(naturally sparkling) ciders in medium-dry, medium, and full bittersweet varieties. My bottled still cider was made without sulphites. (By the way, don't use any fruit other than apple or pear, or add any spices or other flavourings: any of these additives magically and legally transforms your cider into made wine, and all the exemptions you enjoyed as a small cidermaker will disappear). The duty exemption allowed me to sell at a competitive price (in 2017 I retailed my 500ml bottles at £3 (wholesale they would fetch £22 per case of 12, but I sold very little wholesale); 5L bag-in-boxes retailed at up to £20; and 20L bag-in-boxes, which mostly went to pubs, would fetch £40-£50. The big reform of the liquor licensing laws in 2003 mean that you now cannot sell at the farm gate, unless you have both a personal licence and a premises license. You can, however sell at farmers markets and at special occasions if you apply for a Temporary Events Notice (TEN), which you apply for online via your local authority. Up-to-date information on the cider trade can be found on the Weston Cider Report,
https://www.ashdale-consulting.com/wp-content/uploads/2019/04/Weston-Cider-Report-2019.pdf
Learn how to make your own cider by reading the "How to" guide in the appendix at the rear of this book.

Perry

Perry is no more than cider made from pears; and although the word has fallen out of common usage to the extent that many manufacturers of pear-based fruit-flavoured alcoholic drinks describe it as "pear cider", real perry is regarded as a far superior beverage and therefore commands a very worthwhile price premium. One reason why perry fell out of favour was the difficulty of growing the specialised pear varieties that go to make it. Unlike an apple tree, a standard perry pear tree will grow to park size but will take its time

163

in doing so. Anyone who has visited Herefordshire and the counties adjoining, in blossom time (slightly earlier for pears than for apples) cannot have failed to notice the towering and usually solitary specimens absolutely smothered in white bloom. Farmers in these parts used to plant a single tree, because once grown, and it might take fifty years to bear fruit, it would produce sufficient fruit to supply the farm with perry for the year. The slow growth of the tree was, commercially speaking, a fatal handicap. "He who plants pears," it was said, "plants for his heirs". Don't be disheartened at this, because, just like apples, pear scions can be grafted onto quince rootstocks (readily available online), and could be producing fruit within three years, and will always be a more manageable size. Suggested varieties are Blakeney Red, Yellow Huffcap, Littleton Late Treacle or Berllanderi Red.

There is one particular difficulty with perry, however, and that is harvesting and pressing must be undertaken at exactly the right moment. Most varieties have to be picked and milled just before they're perfectly ripe, and not allowed to fall, because they soften quickly, and turn to mush in the mill, clogging the cloths and failing to release juice. My friend, Tom Oliver, introduced me to perry some years ago, and is still regarded as the best commercial perry maker in the UK. Have a look at his website, **www.oliversciderandperry. co.uk**, and learn a little more about this wonderful drink.

Cider Vinegar

Cider vinegar can be made accidentally by allowing air, and with it acetifying bacteria, to come in contact with the cider, or deliberately by setting some of your cider aside (in containers only used for this purpose in a separate building for safety's sake), adding vinegar or a "mother"; i.e. an acetobacter culture, which you can buy at any home brew shop or online, to start the process off, and leaving the tank or vat open to the air covered with gauze or muslin to keep debris and insects out. It can take a few weeks or a few months for all the alcohol to turn to acetic acid, and the resulting vinegar needs to be matured for a time before bottling. As this is a food substance, a best before date is required on all packaging, and Trading Standards at your local authority will give you the details you require.

There is a lucrative market for artisan vinegar, and you can make a profit a third higher than you can on your cider. This popularity is partly due to the health claims it is associated with, and, although none of these claims have been substantiated, it has also been much in demand, especially in the US, during the Covid-19 pandemic. Selling unfiltered apple cider vinegar with an active mother as a starter culture might be another orchard product to add to your smallholding business.

Other opportunities

Your apple trees, pears and other fruit trees produce new growth annually as a matter of course. Most orchardists will simply remove any excess during the winter dormant season and burn the clippings. A few may store these to use to light their fire, for use in barbeques in summer, and some to smoke their own cheese or fish. In this way, even the prunings can be useful, and the tree is totally sustainable. But here are some other money-making ideas to utilise these prunings.

The trees generate valuable scionwood to use for grafting your own trees, (which you could sell in a year or so), or you can sell the scions themselves to others interested in grafting, especially if you have good specimens of known and perhaps hard to source varieties. Just remove good, undamaged lengths of straight, thick young growth and trim to around six to eight inch lengths. Some of the traditional varieties can be very spindly, so search for the thickest ones you can see. Three scion twigs can realise £4 online, and to think you were simply going to use them as kindling! If you "harvest" these during the dormant period a few days before you start pruning, and wrap in wet newspaper, they will store in the fridge for a week or so, to allow you to graft or sell them.

Of course, if you graft your own trees, you can sell these too. Grafting in February should result in trees with good growth by summer. I like to keep them till the following autumn before selling them, to assure myself that the graft is good and strong, before they are bought and planted in a final location. A nice potted two-year-old tree of a heritage or local variety on MM106 will easily fetch £15-£20, and if you produce your own rootstocks and the scion you will only have to lay out for pots and growing medium. Grow my own rootstocks? Yes, indeed, and I'm going to share this well kept little secret with you in the next paragraph!

To produce your own stock of rootstocks, all you will need is a weed-free prepared nursery bed, somewhere sheltered and with good, deep soil. Decide what rootstocks you want to produce. For me, sticking with MM106 was sensible, as these were a popular rootstock for most trees, suitable for commercial growing and medium to large gardens. The rootstocks are fairly disease resistant too, another good selling point. And then you will need to spend a tiny bit of money obtaining some initial rootstocks that will provide you with many years supply by regenerating themselves. Let me explain the process.

Firstly, I order and pay for, say 10 rootstocks from a reputable supplier, which duly arrive in the post. When I unwrap the package I will find 10 small sticks, each with a small amount of fibrous roots and a long stem. How long depends on the

166

supplier, but you could expect rootstocks of a foot long to two foot long. These have been supplied for you, the buyer, to graft your scion onto one of the rootstocks. So far, so good. And here is the secret - as part of the grafting process you will graft your freshly cut scion onto the freshly cut rootstock. The suggested height is six to eight inches above the root ball. And most people will simply cut off the extra, unwanted piece of the top of the rootstock and discard it. However, this is the magic part! This offcut length, if inserted carefully (the right way up) into the prepared nursery bed to a depth of at least 4 inches, will over the next few months, start to root itself and turn into another rootstock! You will know if it has been successful if the bare stick develops leaves in the summer. Any that look like dead, dried up sticks can be gently pulled. If they detach from the soil easily, then they are failures, but I have over 90% success growing my own rootstocks.

Tempting as it may be to sell these baby rootstocks in the coming February, resist. Wait until the following year, and they will have shot up to around three to four feet tall. Cut the rootstock about 9 inches above the soil height and then cut the long length into four or five new twigs to plant for rootstock production. This way your ten original rootstocks have not only created 10 new grafted trees, but the "waste" wood could produce up to 40 new rootstocks.

Amazed as you are by the magical qualities of the apple tree, I have one more gem of knowledge to share with you. The abundance of prunings again never fails to delight me. Yes, there is one more final way to make money from these unwanted prunings and offcuts, and I would have never have believed it until I was sent a message from a friend asking me to post her some apple twigs as a treat for her guinea pigs. Apparently, these are selling on the internet and marketed as natural treats for rodents and cavies, and when I searched online, sure enough, fresh apple twigs are a useful occasional treat, and available to buy online as apple chew sticks.

An orchard is not just a location for fruit trees to grow, but can become an integral part of any garden or farm, to be used in many ways. There is a market for renting fruit trees, especially as memorial trees or for urban families, who fancy having a tree to visit and pick their own fruit, but without the hassle of pruning, etc. Naturally, because you are a busy person, you don't want the public arriving at any old time, so your contract could stipulate a dedicated weekend visiting at blossom time (which you can alert them to about three weeks in advance, again for harvesting their particular tree (again, set a weekend date), and perhaps finally, at Wassail time in January, where you could take advantage of visitors to sell some juice, cider, pork or other produce. For this sort of arrangement, you could easily charge around £50 per tree, and the contract would have to be renewed annually.

December, and the start of the festive season, is the ideal time to sell Christmas themed foliage, and especially mistletoe. Your customers may include those buying at farmers markets and Christmas fairs, but also hotels and restaurants. European mistletoe (Viscum album) is a semi-parasitic plant that lives on apple, poplar and some other species of tree. Popular opinion will tell you that it should be removed or it will kill the host tree, which is untrue. If properly managed and not allowed to grow too large for the host, the two can happily co-exist and provide a useful bit of cash in the bleak midwinter. Both male and female shoots (i.e. berried and unberried) must be pruned, preferably just before the start of the festive season, so the prunings can simply be sold as a crop. Selling mistletoe seeds on the internet in February and March is another niche market. To grow your own mistletoe take at least ten berries off an established plant, carefully remove the seeds from the pulp, and keep them in a light dry place until you're ready to infect a host. Ideally this will be the same species as the host you collected the berries from: if the donor was an apple, then infecting another apple with the berries improves their chances of germinating. Choose a high branch open to the sunlight, and preferably a younger branch 2-6cm in diameter. Infect a spot not too near the trunk by pushing five or six of the seeds (either fresh or dried and then moistened) into the bark on the underside of the branch. A little nick in the bark may help introduce the seed, but is not essential. Leave them exposed or tie them on with a little hessian or grafting tape and expect about one in 10 of them to germinate. With luck you'll see green hypocotyls in six to eight weeks. It's a slow growing plant and can take a few years to establish, so be patient.

Finally, there is the Wassail, or winter folk festival. In the dead of winter, with Christmas a few weeks past, spring can seem to be endlessly distant, but the dark, short days are the perfect excuse for a bit of a party, and this old custom, dating back to at least 1547, is an interesting and fun way to enjoy the orchard in winter. Hot spiced apple juice, cider and hog-roast pork are the order of the day, alongside some traditional music and bizarre costumes. Traditionally, wassails are held on Twelfth Night, but in reality can take place anytime in mid to late January. If you want to make this a commercial event, you'll need a folk group, morris dancers and of course a TEN from your local licensing department. Check the long-range forecast and empty a barn in case the weather catches you out, hire some portaloos, advertise and sell tickets well in advance and enjoy a good night with good cider. A bonfire and torches add to the atmosphere and give light to the proceedings, and as an early evening family shindig, you won't have trouble from badly behaved drunkards.

CASE STUDY -
Dorset Nectar Cider

Oliver & Penny Strong
Strong Orchard
Dorset
www.dorsetnectar.co.uk
Also on FB, Twitter & Instagram

Oliver & Penny Strong didn't originally set out to make cider, but were searching for a home for his sculpting business when in 2006 he bought two barns which came with a 15-acre cider apple orchard. With previous experience in farming and horticulture they were keen to try something new, so they started making cider. With no formal training, they invested their money in the site and equipment, and having nothing left to spend on a family home off-site, took a huge risk and built themselves a small cabin in the orchard. There followed a hard battle with West Dorset District Council for retrospective planning permission, which was finally granted on appeal in 2013.

The orchard, which gained organic status in 2011, has around 3,000 trees, and an annual yield of around 120 tonnes. The Strongs produce their cider in the traditional way, pressing the fruit on two large hydraulic rack and cloth rigs and fermenting the juice with natural yeasts. Marketing is excellent, with an emphasis on customer relations, and despite the Covid-19 pandemic, the company has remained buoyant. Dorset Nectar produces 98% of its income from cider, apple juice, and cider vinegar, with a small income from contract bottling and filtering.

2020 began optimistically, with the introduction of a new bottling line. By March, Covid-19 restrictions forced the end of trade orders, but the family rallied by developing their online shop, and revamping secure packaging for postage. As lockdown eased, demand increased for bottles and pouches of cider, and sales resumed on the farm. Although cider sales were down 40%, the family had survived by keeping its head and promoting its other products, especially cider vinegar. They are keen to introduce champagne cider and apple brandy in the near future.

Quote – "There are always things you'll change along the way, your original plan is not always the way to go, do your research. Dream – it's healthy. Don't hesitate, don't give up. The relationships with your customers and your suppliers are extremely important; if you go the extra mile for them, they will often do the same for you."

Chapter 7
A Wealth of Opportunities

Mainstream farming is used to being criticised as over-intensive, monocultural, and soaked in noxious agrichemicals. Meanwhile extensive farming and adding value have never been an issue for smallholders. Few smallholdings are big enough to be able to farm intensively or make a living out of a single crop, except some very niche crops: most smallholders need more than one string to their bow if they're to make enough money to live on. Either they produce more than one crop off the same land; or they have part-time jobs, often as mechanics, engineers, or lecturers; or they process their own produce, by turning apples into cider, milk into cheese, soft fruit into jam or wine, and live on the value they have added.

You will almost certainly find you need to do the same, even if it's only by getting a hay-crop and some hedge fruit or the rent of a field for car boot sales from April till October. But while there is almost no end to the possible sidelines, marginal opportunities, and secondary income streams that will present themselves, it's important to remain primarily focused on your core business. You only have so much time, energy, and money, so make sure that your lesser ventures don't starve your primary earner of resources. Balance the time and money available to invest in a sideline against the achievable outcome very carefully before settling on a secondary project.

Tourism & Leisure

On a smallholding, every building and every scrap of land has to earn its keep. The cost of renovating or altering redundant farm buildings can be high, although less so if you're capable of doing some of the work yourself, but turning unwanted sheds and barns into active space can prove hugely lucrative in the long run, future-proofing the viability of the whole enterprise.

Farm-based holidays require investment, whether you provide B&B, log cabins, holiday chalets, yurts, shepherd's huts, or caravanning and camping. They also require planning permission, and in the case of camping and caravanning take up land which might well have a more profitable use. But if the value of the pound keeps falling, or travel restrictions become a new way of life, then the delights of the British countryside look likely to be even more attractive to domestic vacationers. Of course it's only during the peak periods – school summer and Easter holidays and term-time bank holiday weekends – that tourism earns top dollar. But you can extend the camping season both forwards and back by a fortnight or more by hosting music, food, and other festivals; and in the off-season the same field could be let out for caravan and boat storage. The more weatherproof accommodation can be kept ticking over off-season by attractive pricing, except at New Year and Valentine's Day. You could also strike a deal with the owner of a local wedding venue to put up entire wedding parties at special rates; more romantic, surely, than a Holiday Inn? You might even have an atmospheric old barn of your own that would make the ideal wedding venue.

You will require a licence, as well as a commercial kitchen with lots of staff and adequate parking and toilets, even if these are temporary. In fact, you would need some sort of staff presence for almost any tourist activity except B&B – seasonal jobs for students and locals alike? Even if you're not in a traditional tourist area you can let surplus outbuildings for a huge range of purposes: there's always a demand for space for self-storage units, yoga and pilates studios, crèches, workshops, offices, shops, auctions, even craft breweries and distilleries.

Another profitable use for surplus outbuildings, or for brand-new purpose-built runs and housing, for that matter is domestic pet boarding. It's a lucrative market, but an expensive one to enter. There are strict criteria regarding size and facilities – proper drainage, electricity, hot and cold water, and sneeze barriers are just a few of them, as well as the handling and welfare of your guests. Word of mouth is just as important as official inspections in keeping you up to the mark, so you have to stay on your toes and not let standards slip. It's a fairly labour-intensive business, too: animals have to be fed, dogs have to be walked, litter has to be changed. You can start charging at £10 a day for basic accommodation for a cat or a small-breed dog and £20 or more for a big-breed dog in a luxury kennel. Animal boarding is regulated by the local authority: you need to apply for a licence and be inspected under the Animal Boarding Act 1963.

Land itself is more versatile than you might suppose. It doesn't have to be planted or grazed: there's a certain demand for outdoor leisure space such as horse livery, dog agility and obedience training, paintballing, archery, clay pigeon shooting, and even allotments.

A few years ago, a canny lady who had a smallholding on the outskirts of Falmouth came up with a fantastic way of making money. She'd been cutting the grass in her field for hay for a few hundred pounds a year when she heard that local residents were demanding that the council should provide them with allotments. It was the push she needed, and she carved up her hay-field into around 100 plots, both full-size and starter. She put some hard standing down for cars and provided a portable loo. Demand outstripped supply, and after three years she bought a neighbouring field to provide more allotments. The allotments are run organically and irrigated with rainwater collected on site, and a communal hut provides somewhere for the allotment holders to gather and chat. Sometimes it's the simplest ideas that work the best and give the best returns.

Field Sports

If you have at least sixty acres of land, but the quality makes it unsuitable for cropping or running livestock, then perhaps concentrating on field sports may be worth considering. Traditional country sports still attract premium clients, but there are opportunities for clay pigeon shooting and traditional shoots aimed at the more middle class markets. Naturally, to make this kind of business a success, experience and knowledge are key. Qualifying as a shooting instructor normally takes around 12 months. For a permanent set up, accessible to large populations you could well have to invest around 350K, as you will require at least 60 acres to ensure planning permission, and permanently sited equipment.

A much cheaper set up would be to run as a mobile clay pigeon shooting operation, offering tuition days, open practice sessions, competitions, stag weekends, corporate events, Christmas present vouchers etc. Tuition only would naturally not generate as much turnover, and open sessions and competitions require the hire of staff to ensure safety. This could be run all year, dependent on the weather and planning permission. A mobile set up would cost around £50K in terms of traps, trailers, stands, safety equipment & guns, and once established could generate a profit of around £12K per annum, so breaking even with this as a solitary project would take a few years. For more information you can contact the Clay Pigeon Association at **www.cpsa.co.uk** or The British Association for Shooting and Conservation at **www.basc.org.uk**.

Game shooting is another alternative, but you will need experience in raising birds or be prepared to pay someone to do this. Not only do you have the same capital investment of land, equipments etc, but also the cost of staff, birds and feed. The profit margins are not high, and therefore you would really be looking at this venture to supplement any existing income stream. For example, on a small syndicate of 16 guns in Devon, each gun paying around £1800, the shoot makes enough to pay for a part time keeper for three months, and the profit would be around £5K if you did this yourself.

Unusual Crops

Any smallholding, particularly as you approach our (admittedly arbitrary) 50-acre upper limit, is going to comprise different sorts of soil suitable for different types of cultivation. And as I said, every scrap of land has to work for its living. By growing some of the more unusual, niche crops, you could have a small, but useful income, especially if you are ideally located for that particular crop.

Turf

Perhaps the most basic sort of crop is plain and simple grass; and what country in the world is as good at growing grass as Britain? With our mild climate and frequent and regular rainfall we revel in glorious gardens, golf courses, meadows, football pitches and even green roofs – all products of the turf industry.

In recent years there has been an explosion of new housing developments, with a corresponding increase in demand for

176

turf for gardens, amenity areas, sports facilities and so on. There is a turf type suitable for all levels of wear, moisture, and light; even lightweight turf for roofing. Naturally, anyone entering this industry will have to have some training or experience whether as a grower, as a green keeper or landscaper. Some private training providers offer suitable courses, and agricultural colleges offer NVQ level 2 courses in sports and amenity turf with Institute of Groundmanship endorsement. Growers have a professional association, the National Turfgrass Council, **www.turfgrass.co.uk**.

Most turf produced in the UK is a mixture of creeping, chewing and red fescues with some rye grass included for robustness, and a good root system to give the turf lateral strength when being cut or laid. Maintenance of the turf includes fertilising, mowing and brushing before harvesting in dry weather with a special turf-cutting machine that rolls the turf into uniform lengths. Production follows an 18-month to two-year cycle, and most growers start with a minimum of 20 acres to cover the costs of machinery and labour. Most growers also produce their own compost to replace the soil lost in harvesting. Turf is a crop like other crops: it requires seeding, maintenance, harvesting, storage, shipping, marketing and replacement. It's also one of the few crops that are happiest in the cooler areas of the north and west.

Christmas trees and Festive foliage

These are a good option for well-drained soil that's not necessarily suited to mechanical cultivation. With a regular planting scheme taking into account that the average Christmas tree takes six to eight years to mature, and noting that trees need to be spaced around 1.2m apart, you could plant around 1500 trees per acre, giving an annual crop of some 187 trees at £30 each or a turnover of £5610 per acre.

Naturally you will need to factor in labour, cost of seedlings (currently under £1 per plant), pesticides and netting.

Skills must be learnt, including basic horticulture, choice of suitable tree variety and provenance, pruning, dealing with insecticide and weedkiller application, and knowing what makes a good tree. This can be mainly learnt by experience, but a good tree will be one–two metres tall, with a classic tapering shape with only small gaps between the branch tiers. While overly lengthy leading shoots in Norway Spruce can be adjusted with secateurs, the leaders in Nordmann Fir will need suppressing with plant growth regulators. The Nordmann Fir has recently had increasing problems with a number of diseases and advice on control of these can be gained by membership of the British Christmas Tree Growers Association (**www.bctga.co.uk**).

Peak times for labour and sales are naturally from the end of November until the week before Christmas, followed by replanting in spring. Herbicidal sprays in the first two years will allow the trees to establish themselves properly, and judicious use of a selective insecticide, such as pirimicarb, will deal with sap-sucking aphids while allowing beneficial insects to flourish.

You can steal a march on the garden centres and supermarkets, who will be your main rivals, partly by undercutting them slightly, but mainly by making the process of choosing and taking away the tree a special and personal occasion. An inviting farm shop selling wreaths and mistletoe as well as trees alongside attractions such as a Santa's Grotto and perhaps a wreath-making workshop (I've done this – it's really easy and very popular), will all attract visitors; and there can be nothing more magical for a child than going up the field with mum, dad and the grower in person, trusty bow-saw in hand, to select that one special tree. Throw in a bit of Santa banter and you can bet they'll be back next year and every year after that!

As for the trees themselves, the old-school Norway Spruce (*Picea abies*) has fallen out of favour and has been largely replaced by species that hold their needles longer and come in different shades. While the most popular tree these days is the Nordmann Fir (*Abies nordmanniana*), with 80% of the market, the Blue Spruce (*Picea pungens glauca*), with its glaucous blue colour is becoming popular, as is the Fraser Fir (*Abies Fraseri*). There are quite a few nurseries where you can buy seedlings, and the return on investment is pretty good if you sell direct to the consumer. For more information visit **www.yctgroup.co.uk** .

Holly and ivy are also good Christmas cash crops, as is mistletoe. I've included more detailed information about mistletoe in the chapter on orchards, so we will touch only on the holly and the ivy here.

Holly is a native British species that has many varieties. Only the female plant produces berries, but you will of course need to plant both sexes if you're going to get a berry crop. It's happy in most soils and situations and only really dislikes very wet soil. You can propagate from hardwood cuttings or indeed graft chosen varieties on to native Ilex aquifolium rootstocks. When choosing varieties you need to look at colour AND sex. This can be quite confusing: Silver Queen with its glossy dark green silver-edged spiky leaves is actually male, and therefore bears no berries, but the spike-free Golden King with lovely red berries is, of course, female. Get both, together with a female native dark-leaved Ilex aquifolium.

For ivy, Hedera helix Goldheart is an excellent foliage plant and will produce long tendrils of variegated green and gold leaves. Silver Queen (a different Silver Queen!) has variegated green and white leaves. Christmas wreaths can be made quickly and quite simply with a ring of willow (make these up in the spring), with holly and ivy entwined round it, finished off with a red or gold bow and maybe a pine cone or bauble or two. They'll fetch £4-£8, so there isn't a huge profit in them, but they're incremental to the tree sale, and you can also sell the decorative greenery to florists, pubs, hotels, and restaurants.

Lavender

The familiar blue-to-mauve aromatic shrub, and its cousin lavandin, named for their age-old use in scenting fresh laundry, are high-value crops for the cosmetics industry, with dried flowers and oil being the two saleable products. Growing them is becoming increasingly popular, especially among cereal farmers seeking to diversify.

Fields of lavender have one great advantage over most other crops: they are stunningly beautiful. This makes them an attraction in their own right, on the back of which you can build a retail business, specialising in the many manifestations of the lavender itself as well as all the other goods you (and perhaps your neighbours) produce. Products such as lavender and lavandulin bags and pillows are eternally popular; and lavender can be combined with hops or wheat for microwaveable muscle soothers. Offering plants for sale is an obvious option, and a multitude of culinary uses include infusion in dry sugar or syrup to flavour cream, cake filling, butter, icing, chocolate, ice cream, sorbet, meringues, vodka – almost anything, really. Traditional herbs de Provence includes lavender as part of the mix. It can be used with honey as a glaze for roast duck, or with chocolate for venison. And try infusing it with apricots to make a heady Mediterranean jam!

It's a great convenience that lavender is in full bloom at the height of summer, evoking Provence just when there are most likely to be tourists about. Open days with tours and picnics are therefore more or less guaranteed to generate a large income, although given the unpredictability of the British summer the need for staff, parking, toilet facilities and shelter areas represent quite an investment. Allowing the fields to be used for commercial photography and filming is a lucrative bonus, too.

Lavender requires sunny, warm, well-drained, light, alkaline soil, preferably with chalk or lime content, and, in the UK, is frequently planted through polythene or weed-mat, as you can't use herbicidal sprays on crops destined for culinary, pharmaceutical or cosmetic use. (For added kerb-appeal, you can mulch the rows of lavender nearest your shop or café with bright white sand and/or crushed oyster shell between the rows). Harvesting replaces pruning, so there's no double-handling. The plants will last for eight or nine years before they have to be replaced. Different varieties suit different purposes. *Lavandula angustifolia* produces a high-quality essential oil suitable for perfumes and *L. Intermedia* (technically a lavandin, not a lavender), produces around 50% more essential oil but of a lesser quality, more suited to soap and massage oil, aromatherapy, and pot pourri oil. Both have antiseptic qualities. To produce dry lavender, the flowers are harvested when the first couple of buds on the stem have opened. Long-stemmed lavender makes perfect decorative bunches, while shorter stems are ideal for drying for pot pourri and pillows. Your rain shelter building or café ceiling space may double up as pretty drying areas.

The oil is extracted by steam distillation: the tops are seethed in boiling water or live steam until it evaporates, and is carried off to condense in a tank, where the lighter oil sits on top of the water and can then be drawn off for packaging. A realistic yield from varieties such as Mailette and Folgate of around 40 litres an acre can fetch upwards of £50 a litre;

Grosso lavandin can yield double that amount but realises only £20 a litre.

Cut flowers and decorative foliage

Traditional favourites such as chrysanthemums and carnations have taken a beating since the 1960s, and there are only a few producers left. Daffs and narcissi are still popular, though, both as bulbs and cut flowers. The South-West, the Scillies and the Channel Islands, where mild winters and early springs promote early growth and satisfy demand for spring flowers, have always been the main centres of production, but Bedfordshire and other traditional centres of market gardening are important centres too, where the budding horticultural entrepreneur will still find good growing conditions, networks of suppliers, and access to markets.

The British cut-flower market is worth £2.2bn retail, of which 90% is channelled through supermarkets; but there's increasing demand from the hospitality and wedding trades, as well a growing corporate market for fresh displays in prestige offices and at promotional events. This, coupled with climate change, has seen British growers challenge the dominance of importers, and the acreage devoted to flowers has expanded by more than 30% in the past five years. Unfortunately the prices are dictated by multiple retailers who can of course sell flowers at cut-throat prices, but the customer is demanding (and getting) an ever-wider variety of ornamentals, including hebes, eucalyptus, ivies, and winter-flowering specials such as witch hazel, corkscrew hazel, and phormium leaves. Relatively new entrants into the cut flower market include sunflowers, lilacs, hydrangeas, sweet peas, and British wild flowers such as sweet rocket and foxgloves; and domestic growers are exploiting the fact that British flowers retain their scent better than forced foreign imports to make the local choice more attractive and worth that little bit extra.

Most cut-flower producers are big, heavily-capitalised enterprises with large overheads in chemicals, heating and mainly seasonal labour. But I know some smallholders in Cornwall who have made good returns from growing cut flowers and greenery on less than an acre, requiring no more than a polytunnel for the more delicate blooms, applying no chemicals, and hiring no pickers. By using harvested rainwater, biomass boilers or solar panels, production costs can be slashed and the normal growing season can be extended.

Willow

Traditional willow and hazel baskets have become popular decorative items both in the home, and in the retail and hospitality trades. Working creatively with willow has expanded into landscape design, furniture making, and living sculpture. Our heightened awareness of sustainability has even led us to choose willow coffins as a way to make an emphatic final statement.

Willows are our fastest-growing and highest-yielding tree or shrub and are particularly suited to cool and damp conditions. They are also very versatile. The long, strong, slender, flexible twigs or withies are plaited and then twisted round the harder, thicker sticks to make trugs and baskets of all shapes and sizes, elegant outdoor or indoor furniture, hurdles, screens, blinds and 101 other things. They come in many colours, too, to fire your imagination yet further. The setts or cuttings can also be sold to gardeners, as can bundles of sticks and withies for hobby basket-makers.

Another market is giving talks or exhibitions of your work and offering courses on basketry or making, Christmas wreaths or garden sculptures. Many Christmas fairs, country craft markets, and agricultural shows even employ willow weavers to run drop-in events where children and parents can make a small basic item to take home. Take advantage of the long, dark evenings of winter and early spring to build up a stock of top-quality items for sale at shows, craft fairs, or online. Costs are minimal but weaving is a laborious process (until you get used to it) and retail prices aren't high, so only direct sales of premium products will make you a worthwhile profit.

Willow rods grow from a stump-like stool, which take about three years from planting to harvesting. The beds are harvested in winter when bare, and each stool can produce up to 30 rods or wands, of around eight feet long. They are easy to grow and require little input. Willow and other similar coppice have more uses than producing baskets and rods, and many are employed as a biodegradable river bank support structure to prevent soil erosion.

Short rotation coppicing is a quick and efficient method of producing wood for fuel, either as whole logs (taking around five years), or woodchip (around three) for biomass boilers. Good varieties to grow include *Salix viminalis gigantea* or *S. viminalis Bowles Hybrid*. A five-year short rotation coppice planted 1m apart in 1.5m spaced rows will produce around six tonnes of firewood an acre every five years. Take precautions to keep grazers out, as all animals like willow. You will also need storage space to dry the wood.

Pharmaceutical crops

You may not know it, but pharmaceutical crops are quite widely grown around Britain, often on quite small plots and in total secrecy, under the guardianship of private companies retained by the government. Often the reward for a contract with one of these companies is not great; but then the contractor usually carries out the harvest on security grounds. Opportunities in this field may be rare, but are still worth enquiring after.

The opium poppy, *Papaver somniferum*, has been a legal crop in the UK since 2002, when there was a worldwide shortage of opiates; and today there are fields of rather mysterious mauve and lilac flowers dotted around Oxfordshire, Northamptonshire, Dorset and Lincolnshire, where the light soils suit their cultivation. The contractor for opium poppies is Scottish drug company Macfarlan Smith, which licenses growers on around 7,000 acres around the country. The yield should be around 15kg a hectare, which is worth £1,000 to the farmer. Not bad for a spring-sown break-crop!

Taxus baccata (English yew, Irish yew and Golden yew) is infamous because all parts of the tree are poisonous. However, the needles also produce the taxanes used to treat cancer and are harvested between May and October. Friendship Estates in Doncaster collects and pays for annual clippings. For details contact **www.friendshipestates.co.uk**.

Using polytunnels for multiple uses is a clever and good financial use of resources. Remember what I said at the end of chapter 1 about a work-wheel and working out what you were doing at certain times of the year? A large polytunnel used for lambing (and drying laundry) in winter/early spring, could also double up as an exotics production centre from mid spring onwards. One farmer who does just this is Ian Paxton, who uses his tunnels for growing chillies, which are ready to harvest in September and October. He has produced a really nice little YouTube video here which explains why and what he grows **https://youtu.be/UhE624jjzZo**

To dry chillies you can string them onto strong thread (through the green part just down from the stem) and hang in a well ventilated area or hang from that drying pulley

above the wood-burner; basically anywhere where the air is dry and warm. Drying takes three to four weeks. For using different parts of the chilli for different products I found this little video very informative
https://youtu.be/eT0c0MDSUt0

There are many varieties of chilli and you will need to grow the ones that sell the best, obviously. Heat is not the most important factor – lots of customers routinely use chillies to give flavour to Asian, Mexican and Jamaican dishes. Fresh and dried chillies, and chilli dipping sauces and in olive oil are all popular both online and for sale at markets and food fairs. Chillies need some heat to propagate and when growing need at least six hours of sunlight to start fruiting. In southern areas you can start seed off indoors in January to harvest in July; further north you would be better waiting till March. Growing chillies as small plug plants (Jiffy 7 size with around 5 leaves) for selling on the internet is another option. If demand is small then the plants can be potted on and sold at food fairs and markets. A really good book on chilli growing is the *RHS Red Hot Chilli Grower* by Kay Maguire (2015).

Another exotic with a big commercial pull is Wasabi. This hot flavoured root hails from the east and is finding increasing prominence in both Asian and European restaurants. As a native from Japan it can be grown in shady and very moist conditions, and possibly suitable outdoors with shading in the South Western side of the UK. With a bed of ever-damp gravel, small scale production of this very profitable vegetable can be achieved if the grower protects the crops from slugs and caterpillars. It will grow in ordinary soil if shaded, but you won't get the swollen root unless you grow in damp (not wet) soil. You can crop the leaves and the swollen root. Roots can command £200 plus per kilo.

Pet and Bird Food

This sector is fast-growing and offers many alternative crops and products for anyone willing to do a little research and take some risks. Millet, maize and sunflowers are in increasing demand for the bird seed. In 2012 the market was worth £200 million and it's grown since then. It's part of a market for prepared pet foods of all sorts, that's worth £1.5 billion, but it's a highly regulated one. Before you start you have to register with your local authority and if your products contain any ingredients of animal origin (e.g. milk, honey, meat, or fish), then you also need approval from APHA and the Veterinary Laboratories Agency. There are strict rules about hygiene during manufacture and about labelling. See EU Regulation (EC) 183/2005 and EU Regulation (EC) 767/2009. More information can be found at **www.pfma. org.uk/uk-pet-food-legislation**.

Contracting, Seasonal, & relief work

Many smallholders make extra cash by hiring out their services to other smallholders, or even mainstream farmers either at busy times, or as specialists in one field or another, or as sickness/holiday cover. If you find that there are times when you had some spare capacity, this is a good way of earning some ready money and is also, crucially, the foundation of a business and social network in a sphere of operations where isolation can be a terrible affliction.

At harvest time or whenever staff and machinery are stretched, relying on contractors is cheaper than hiring or buying. Traditional seasonal jobs such as cutting and topping paddocks, ploughing, hedging and ditching, hay cutting and baling, and fencing and timber work are also often contracted out, and then there are one-off jobs such as removing dung heaps and muckspreading.

Although the work may be unpredictable, agricultural contracting might suit a semi-retired farm worker, or a smallholder with other income streams as well. And smallholders themselves often use contractors for smaller jobs that don't justify the expense of buying specialised equipment. Hourly rates start at around £25 depending on the job and the machinery required: visit **www.naac.co.uk**.

Lambing

The traditional lambing season has been extended thanks to new breeding techniques, and help with lambing, especially at night, is now in demand from late November until mid-April. For a lambing nightshift of 8-12 hours you could expect to be paid £10-£12 per hour. It's not a life-changing amount of money, unless you are extremely skilled or prepared to work in a remote area. As lambing can be expected to take place both indoors in barns or outbuildings, or out in the open field, it makes sense to clarify this before accepting such a role. Remember that there is a risk to any female lambing staff who are, or think they may be, pregnant (see the section on sheep in the Livestock chapter).

Mobile shearing

With the right skills you can also offer a mobile shearing service for other smallholders. Most large sheep farms hire the travelling shearers from Australia and New Zealand, who will only cater for flocks of 200 upwards. The smallholder with 10 sheep that need shearing often struggles to find a shearer, but the job has to be done for the sheep's welfare, and this presents a fantastic opportunity for someone fit and healthy, with experience, who is prepared to travel about to small jobs. The rate at time of writing is about £2 a beast, but you should agree a minimum charge plus fuel to make it worth your while.

Relief milking

As a part-time service offered as holiday or sickness cover, a normal four-hour milking shift should pay £40-£50. You will need enough experience to be trusted to work on your own.

Milk recording

This requires meticulous accuracy in taking samples from dairy cows. You need your own transport and will be paid a set rate with travel expenses which works out to about £12 per hour. Most milk recorders work on a self-employed basis for a company called National Milk Records, which collects information on individual animals' milk yield and quality and fertility. The recorder visits monthly to take samples. Farm visits last a couple of hours each.

Drystone walling

Stone walls built without mortar or cement are common in the UK where stone is plentiful but wood is scarce, and can be seen all over Great Britain and Ireland, with different local styles evolved from the types of stone available. In Cornwall, for instance, the wall is hollow and filled with soil and small stones known as shillet, topped with a living hedge. Drystone walls make durable and attractive boundary markers, field enclosures, and animal shelters. In the dim distant past the technique was also used to build sheds, barns, pigsties, even whole cottages, many of which can still be seen in rocky upland country. More recently there has been a large revival of interest in drystone walling as a more enduring, cost-effective and sustainable method of enclosure than fencing.

Any waller will warn you that you need a special quality to succeed in the craft: an appetite for long hours of hard graft on your own in all weathers in the middle of nowhere. You also need experience and training: you may have started out repairing sections on your own holding, progressed to helping out your neighbours, and then decided to train properly in the art. There are training providers all over the country such as **www.wallsforthefuture.co.uk**, through Lantra, **www.lantra.co.uk**, or the Drystone Wallers Association, **www.dswa.org.uk**.

The work itself is slow and painstaking and demands intense concentration to ensure that whatever the job on hand, whether new-build or repair, it's done thoroughly, safely, and with an eye for detail that will produce a wall both sturdy and in keeping with the local style. It's got to be right, too: you don't want to be coming back! A proficient drystone waller should be able to complete 3-4m^3 a day, depending on the weather, so fix your daily rate accordingly. (Only the National Trust and English Heritage are likely to pay by the hour). A typical charge would be £100 per m^3 if you're supplying the stone, £60 if you're not. But be warned: you will face competition from semi-professionals – landscape gardeners and the like, who will undercut you ruthlessly, especially on the smaller patching-up jobs. Part of your pitch should therefore be that the prospective client has two choices: pay the cheapjack rate now and your rate in a year or two's time, or pay your rate now and nothing more for a century!

Smallholding Sitting Services

A useful service for smallholders, horse owners and even just dog owners, is that of the smallholder sitter. We all need someone reliable and knowledgeable to occasionally come to the rescue if we have an emergency, or a short absence from the farm or smallholding. Well-meaning friends or family are not always the best people to hand over the keys to, as they may not have any experience in what is required day to day. I remember the look on my townie brother's face when I asked him to come and housesit, and look after two dogs, two cats and a few chickens. The responsibility of creatures he'd never looked after frightened him immensely. House and farm sitting is always in demand, and if you can obtain good references and insurance for this, it offers a nice little earner in locations all over the UK if you are prepared to travel.

Farm accounting services

Rural businesses and smallholders are all very busy people, usually lacking comprehensive accounting knowledge. I used to do all my own accounts when I ran a very simple business, but as the business grew and incorporated many projects, I enlisted the services of a proper accountant to help me consolidate my books and take advantage of all methods to retain as much turnover as possible. A good accountant should be able to save you money!

Completing a City & Guilds Level 3 Rural Business Administration and then getting IagSA affiliation offers many bookkeepers an excellent opportunity to incorporate the completion of farm business accounts for both their own business and as a service to smallholders, farmers and other rural businesses.

Jessica Pillow's rural accounting firm is unlike any other. Her business, Pillow May (**www.pillowmay.co.uk**) operates out of a farmhouse in the south of England. She knows that a practical understanding of agriculture and rural businesses helps her connect with rural business owners. Her staff are all mums, and work life balance is important to them, so flexible working is key.

Jessica and her staff specialise in rural accounting. She grew up on a large farm in Hampshire, England and her father managed the family farm. Jessica has always been inspired by her parents' ability to balance work and family life – and it echoes in her own business. With the recent developments in IT and cloud technology, it's easier than ever to set up your own business. It can be demanding working with small businesses, but the rewards are worth the hard work.

Website Design

Another skill that can be brought from an earlier career is website design. As a marketing tool, every business really needs an online presence and a website is accessible to those who have yet to explore the worlds of social media. I attended a four day course to learn how to make my own website on Wordpress, and although I found the tuition intense, once I started using the software, I became very happy with it and could link it to social media, run competitions, newsletters and gain data from it.

To offer web design as a business you really need a fair bit of experience; not necessarily qualifications. Some knowledge of your client's product area and audience and of the competition will be of huge benefit. As a web designer there is really not much in the way of outgoings at all if you have an existing computer. You need to be able to extract from your client a pretty accurate brief (which can be time consuming), and work quickly and efficiently. Once you have completed the brief to your client's satisfaction, you need to move on to the next job with fresh eyes and new ideas. So, little outgoings, large market; what's the catch? Well, as a home-based business, there is a lot of competition out there, and clients can be very hard to pin down to extract what style, content, features they want when they have never had a website before. If you are considering this as a business option, you should consider having "set" packages as options for your clients, perhaps offer an update service for two hours monthly at a set price, and finally, ensure that your clients know you work strict business hours and don't work out-with these.

Soap making

This can be done at a very small scale at home, in a workshop or indeed larger premises. Common sense would suggest that you begin soap making as a hobby until you perfect your skill and recipes and can fairly evaluate the possibility of turning this into a business. Then, if you want to start commercially you should be researching your market and how and what you are going to sell. With a relatively low priced product you will need to sell a substantial amount of soap to make any sort of reasonable wage from it. This means spending as little time as possible on the soap making process by being efficient, and concentrating on marketing and selling. Products currently in high demand are handmade wedding favour packages and Christmas gift packages.

There are two main ways to manufacture soap – hot process and cold process. Hot process making was the traditional way to make soap starting centuries ago, and the final product is ready to use as soon as the soap is made. Nowadays most people use cold process soap making which can take weeks to allow the lye and fat to transform into soap. Either method requires considerable outlay for production and packaging if you wish to sell products, so you need to weigh up the pros and cons of starting this as a business and whether it will make enough profit for your needs. You may want to consider registering the business as a PLC or LLP to offer some protection against litigation, but at the very least you should definitely get product liability insurance, which may cost you around £300 annually.

Secondly, there is a lot of red tape to work through in order to legally sell soap in the UK. The manufacture and sale of soaps and toiletries is governed by the **EU Cosmetics Regulation No 1223/2009**. This is applicable to anyone selling soap irrespective of the size or scale of your business and you must be in compliance with the legislation when you accept money for your products. If you ensure you comply you can sell your soaps anywhere in the EU.

As a manufacturer you must hold a safety assessment for any soaps you are selling within the EU, which must be undertaken by a "suitably qualified professional person" who has to sign off each soap recipe made for sale. It's crucial to ensure that he or she is knowledgeable and experienced and covered by Professional Indemnity Insurance, which will provide protection for you should any litigation be brought against you if someone experiences an adverse reaction to your soaps. The completed assessment is valid indefinitely. The Department for Business Innovation and Skills and Trading Standards provide in-depth information on the regulations. More information can be found here **http://www. cosmeticsafetyassessment.com**. There are many companies which supply courses to help you towards regulatory compliance and some of these can also undertake safety assessments. Try **www.aromantic.co.uk** who have loads of courses and information on setting up small businesses. All of this sounds like a massive and difficult process to go through, but recently certifying chemists have been allowed to pass groups of recipes, rather than each single recipe.

You are also required to have a Product Information File (PIF) which should contain information similar to that required for the safety assessment including labelling details, the weight and pH of each soap, batch records and traceability of ingredients. This file should be kept in a safe place and made available for scrutiny on request.

Blacksmithing

There are very few full-time blacksmiths in the UK and one reason is that hand forged decorative items take longer to fabricate than mass produced, and therefore cannot compete with inferior machine-made items from the far East. According to the British Artist Blacksmiths Association **www.baba.org.uk**, there are more blacksmiths working today than there were thirty years ago, but this doesn't mean that they work full-time, or that they are running their forge as a business. Many are part-timers or retired and doing the business as a hobby. Many people calling themselves blacksmiths are really metal workers who buy in component parts and weld or fire-weld these together. This will make their finished products cheaper, but basically you get what you pay for.

Traditional blacksmiths can basically fabricate all sorts of metal, but mainly steel and occasionally wrought iron and copper. Instead of traditional farm implements, weaponry and workmen's tools, you are far more likely to see modern blacksmiths making jewellery, garden furniture or repairing church or heritage ironmongery. There are private tutors who can teach to a certain level, but the main centres for training are found at Warwickshire College and Hereford College of Technology.

My husband John is a blacksmith, as was his father, who was also a farrier. They are not one and the same. A farrier shoes horses, but needs training in blacksmithing to make horseshoes; a blacksmith fabricates other things, and usually never has contact with horses. John built a solid business repairing gates and railings, doing heritage work for local churches, and some artistic commissions such as candle sconces and candlesticks etc, but his main income was from teaching. Because of health and safety he taught a maximum of two people at any time, as it's hard to keep an eye on two pupils and a forge all at once. His equipment included a coke forge with electric blower, a couple of anvils, vices and an array of tongs and tools. I should add that his brain was his most important asset. You really need to think in a different way when you are making anything out of metal.

When the weather is cold it's a great job to keep warm, but he can be dripping in sweat in the summer, which is when most people want to come for courses. Tuition insurance for such a subject is pricey but essential, and this has to be passed on as part of the tuition fee. A normal teaching day starts at 10am, finishes around half past four with a half hour for lunch and resting your hammer arm. It's very physical and dirty, but immensely popular, and one of the five most endangered crafts in the UK today.

CASE STUDY –
Coddington Christmas Trees

Colin Palmer
Ledbury
Herefordshire
www.festive-Ledbury.co.uk
www.ruralservices.info

After a spell studying agriculture, Colin Palmer spent many years working in the agrochemical sector; including a 20 year spell with Shell Chemicals where he had responsibility for pesticide training and product development. In 1974 he bought a three-acre smallholding and set up Coddington Christmas Trees, growing and selling Christmas trees, and Rural Services, a company offering advice and training on weed, pest and disease control in forestry and Christmas trees.

The plot, set in woodland at an altitude of 160m, included a derelict 1830s house with no vehicular access of its own, which was being used as animal housing and was at risk of demolition. After a planning wrangle, Colin was finally able to renovate it and has also replaced the old timber barn with a modern steel building suitable for his agricultural and forestry business.

The sales window is only three to four weeks annually, but Colin is kept busy throughout the year. He is frequently asked if Christmas trees would make a good crop for people with small areas of land; his 2016 book *Christmas Trees - A Growers Guide* (ISBN 9781897781418, 2016) aims to give the answer.

Strong marketing skills are the most important skill to learn, says Colin. Produce an attractive marketing campaign with the best photographs you can get. Then learn the associated skills and plan for a long wait (six to eight years) till your first trees are ready to harvest and sell. Investigate other seasonal crops to maximise your takings, such as mistletoe or seasonal greenery, Christmas wreaths and Christmas tree stands etc. Pot grown trees command an increasing share of the market annually (now approaching 10%), but require precise watering & maintenance throughout the growing period; and the choose-your-own market is also increasing.

Chapter 8
Education and Teaching

When I was a Training Co-ordinator for the Rural Business School in Cornwall, I found that among the students were a number of working farmers and growers who wanted to expand their knowledge of a wide range of subjects both at certificated and uncertificated levels. You do require formal qualifications for some areas of work on the holding, but by no means for all, and some people just feel happier having a certificate even if they don't actually require one. We all have to accept that we can't learn everything, but to master the skills we lack we may have to pay someone else for their expertise. And who better to pay than someone who's done it all not once but every day – maybe someone like you?

The right stuff

There's a steady demand for courses in horticulture, agriculture, animal husbandry and other rural skills, many of which are taught formally in classrooms in community colleges and other similar venues, but many of which can't be taught in conventional settings. After all, you can't really demonstrate how to kill and prepare a chicken for the oven in a classroom!

You may wish to sign up to teach a part-time or evening course at a local college; but if you have the appropriate

199

facilities, including parking, toilets and somewhere that could be used as a classroom, and a subject that people are eager to learn, then teaching this can be a good business. Teaching is a flexible skill. It may be one-to-one or one to one hundred; it can be a lecture, a practical demonstration, a day course, or a set of classes over a few weeks. Each situation is as different and as unique as each learner.

The snide old saying "those that can – do, and those that can't – teach" couldn't be further from the truth: teaching is a skill that most providers have to learn. A good teacher will engage their learners with interesting and informative lessons, and be able to measure the learners' knowledge both at the start, and at the end of a lesson; that doesn't just happen by chance. A lot of work goes into lesson planning, with a variety of teaching styles included because we all learn differently. Some of us like to read to learn, others to watch a video or demonstration; others prefer to act out or practice a task physically. Some of us learn better on our own and others in groups, and a good lesson will try to cover a subject in a variety of activities and tasks.

As a result teaching is a great responsibility. It's tiring and demanding, and if you mess up then your failure is horribly visible. We can all have off days, but if teaching is your livelihood then negative feedback, or worse still negative feedback on social media, will seriously affect your ability to attract new students. Being professional and business-like has to be the order of the day, from putting a course together and making sure your professional paperwork is both in order and valid, to delivering appropriate teaching.

Good teachers need more than subject knowledge, suitable premises, and time. Effective communication and interpersonal skills are essential. If you don't like people then you're going to struggle, and both you and your learners are going to have a less than perfect experience. You also need the confidence to remain calm and professional especially when things don't go to plan. Organisational skills are of critical importance – it's up to you to ensure your learners know where, when and what they are doing; you need to plan what you intend to deliver and have any activities, handouts, demonstrations, props etc, in place.

Examine what relevant prior experience you have – a career in the services, or in a supervisory or management role, for example, or even in raising a family, will have given you the qualities that enable you to teach, tutor, or coach. Organisational and managerial skills, though, should be deployed to enhance rather than overshadow that all-important virtue of flexibility. Not all learners learn at the same pace or to the same level. This can lead to conflict; which you as the teacher, need to control and defuse. You need to motivate and reward *all* your learners, and be able to empathise and encourage when they just don't get it despite your best efforts. Also, you need to remember that, unlike school students, adult learners often have complicated lives, and may have issues with childcare, finance, or health.

Adult learning

Most of the teaching within agriculture, horticulture and rural skills is aimed at adults. While there is demand among younger people, informal providers such as a farm-based instructor will have problems getting the appropriate insurance. As a result, it tends to be schools that offer learning opportunities within the national curriculum's environmental and land-based science syllabus. Other learning providers for youngsters include National Federation of Young Farmers' Clubs, **www.nfyfc.org.uk**, which also run Train the Trainer events (TTT) for anyone who would like to try their hand at teaching.

Your learners will therefore be adults, who are well-motivated and have high expectations of you. However, they are all individuals with different levels of experience, different levels of education, and different amounts of time they can devote to learning. By clearly defining the level you are offering, together with information such as start and finishing times, how many sessions the course includes, and whether there will be any homework, you will help your aspiring learners to choose the most suitable course for their needs and circumstances.

Here, as an example, are the different courses and syllabuses you might offer to cover a single subject, in this case beekeeping.

- An introductory "beekeeping experience" might be a short taster suitable for all levels of interest, perhaps combining a visit to an apiary with some discussion of what beekeeping was all about. The session would last two to three hours, and there would be no handouts or notes.
- A beginners' course would possibly last six hours, with a short practical session with the bees and longer spent in a classroom with handouts and possibly a slideshow or Powerpoint presentation.
- An intermediate beekeeping course might consist of eight two-hour sessions with notes, homework, some practical experience, and some kind of test at the end either with or without certification.

For learners with absolutely no experience, the introductory session provides the learner with basic information about what is entailed and a practical session without committing either time or expense. If it transpires that the learner is

202

terrified of bees, or is claustrophobic in the bee-suit, then nothing is lost. A short, cheap, no-strings intro of this sort is very popular, with many learners, and represents an income-stream even if many of the candidates decide not to progress. Those who progress to the beginners' course should expect to learn enough to take up beekeeping as a hobby, and the intermediate course to turn a hobby into a business. The tutor or teacher in this case had better know their stuff and should also be prepared to tailor their teaching to the learners' needs.

On-site Teaching

What you can teach on your own premises depends not only on your own knowledge and experience, but also on the facilities you have. Our smallholding had an orchard, we kept bees and chickens, we reared bottle-fed lambs, and we made cider. John had a working forge and two welding bays. That meant we could teach beekeeping, chicken keeping, practical lambing, orchard skills, cidermaking, blacksmithing, and welding.

Your own ambitions as a teacher will be determined to some extent, as ours were, by the limitations of your holding, but there are other factors to take into account too. Researching what subjects and courses are already on offer in the area is the obvious first step.

John was the only private welding instructor for over 100 miles, so he had quite a few learners over the years and was also a tutor for the Rural Business School. His one-day beginners' workshops in blacksmithing proved very popular as Christmas and birthday gifts – a handy marketing tip for you there! On the other hand the growing popularity of community apple groups offering very cheap tuition limited the number of pruning workshops I could fill, although I could run two cidermaking workshops in October because there was no other provision in the area. All in all we did very well out of seasonal courses and made some great friends over the years.

Hosting courses on your smallholding is less formal and undeniably more fun than holding evening classes in the more formal surroundings of your local community college. But it is no less demanding of your teaching skills and of the diligent preparation of course materials. If you are giving a talk or a presentation, then you have little option but to have a stationary audience and not much interaction, so I always liked to script-in opportunities to ask the students a question or two as we went along. This would let me know how well they were following and reassure me that they hadn't fallen asleep!

Sometimes at the end of a talk I would produce samples, which always went down well when I was teaching cidermaking. A variety of suitable props, and tasks that the students actually had to carry out, had great illustrative value. The climax of my one-day chicken-keeping course, for example, was humane dispatch. I offered this both in council-run leisure classes and for the Rural Business School, and was well aware that not every prospective chicken keeper was keen on the idea of dispatch at all. However, I believe animal owners need to accept responsibility for their livestock, and be able to humanely euthanize any as a result of injury, illness or predator attack. As the day edged towards the end, the atmosphere would become very serious and one or two learners would often ask to be excused. Then I'd reveal my secret prop – a rubber chicken bought at a pet shop. Not only did it lighten the atmosphere, but I actually used it to demonstrate humane slaughter without making anyone sick.

Talks

Community teaching is another avenue you may wish to explore. Organisations such as Women's Institutes and gardening clubs customarily hire evening speakers. An hour-long talk which may include a Powerpoint presentation or slide-show and appropriate props, should net you around £50 and is also good practice. An hour is a long time to keep the attention of an audience, so you need to break it up for the sake of variety.

I put together a presentation on cidermaking for local gardening groups which started with a comparative tasting of dessert and cider apples, followed by a 20-minute slide-show, and concluded with a tasting of cider. This broke the presentation down into neat sections – an appetiser, a main and a dessert, if you will – that held the audience's attention, with a final Q&A session standing in for coffee and cigars. The cost to me was a few apples and a couple of bottles of cider. The resources for the talk were all kept in a file, and I must have made at least £1,000 from taking it down off the shelf every autumn. If you fancy doing talks, you need to contact your groups at least a year in advance and tell them what you do, your price and what you require, e.g. a socket, a table, and a white wall.

Qualifications

As we have seen, I could teach a fairly wide range of subjects on the basis of experience alone; but that doesn't mean I had no qualifications. When I started teaching horticulture for Cornwall Adult Education, I had one Level 3 Award in horticulture and another in education and training, which was enough to allow me to start formal teaching in the Lifelong Learning Sector. I also began work as a part-time tutor for the Rural Business School, which offered short courses or training in rural skills, agriculture, and horticulture.

Working for both organisations increased my confidence and competency in teaching, and provided me with a suitable classroom or workshop, and, most importantly, insurance. If you are thinking of teaching, this route is one I would recommend before you begin to search for insurance to teach from your own premises. Another benefit of working for a college is that you are instructed how to write risk assessments, lesson plans etc. You can attend classes and learn from other teachers, as well as benefiting from in-house training such as Continued Professional Development. All this will be invaluable when you are preparing your own courses or workshops.

Risk Assessments

Risk assessments are essential if you're preparing to teach outside a classroom or engage in an activity with animals, equipment or tools. Classroom-based learning is already pre-assessed by the college or council to cover such potential risks as projectors, cables, computer screens and so forth, so that a tutor just has to check the RA, check cables and trip hazards and tell learners to keep their bags under the table for the same reason.

Outside the classroom it's a different matter. A risk assessment may include a range of other considerations. If you have learners with physical or mental impairment then your risk assessment is going to be more detailed still, and you may find you need a learning support assistant who will require details of the learner's particular needs. The more complex or dangerous the course or activity might be, the more detailed the risk assessment. That doesn't mean the activity can't go ahead, it just means that you should be able to show you were prepared to deal with whatever might crop up. They all cover:

- Identifying hazards (i.e. anything that may cause harm whether physical, mental, chemical or biological)
- Deciding who may be harmed and how (i.e. teacher/learners or all, especially noting young, disabled or vulnerable)
- Assessing the risks (how likely/how severe) and taking preventative action
- Recording all the above
- Reviewing at least every six months or when equipment is introduced or removed or conditions change.

This example is for a college apple juicing course.

RISK ASSESSMENT EXAMPLE –APPLE JUICING

Hazard or harm	Who is at risk	How are risks currently controlled	Are additional control measured needed
Weight of equipment/apples – risk of strain through lifting. Risk of equipment falling over onto operators.	Learners, tutor.	Lift only as instructed and with care, using help if necessary. Ensure mill & press are set up correctly and on a level surface.	No
Hygiene – contamination risk from machinery	End consumer of juice products.	Wash/sterilize all equipment prior to use. Ensure press operator takes precautions to avoid contamination of pulp with dirty hands.	No

Contamination risk from dirty/ rotten fruit	End consumers, learners, tutor.	Remove all rotten fruit, foreign bodies. Wash all fruit in regularly changed clean water. Remind users that juice is NOT pasteurised and therefore must be refrigerated/used within four days	No
Contamination risk from containers	End consumer	All new and reused containers must be clean/ sterilised.	No
Contamination risk from dirty clothing/footwear/ hands of operators	End consumer	Ensure participants follow rules for clean clothing, footwear and wash hands regularly throughout event. Continual supervision of press whilst in operation.	No
Mill use risks – electric shock.	Learners, tutor.	Ensure mill is PAT tested, use RCD device, avoid wetting machinery, do not use with wet hands.	No
Trip hazard, mill blade injury to hands.	Learners, tutor.	Arrange cables to avoid trip hazard. Ensure hopper is bolted onto mill prior to use. Do not overload with fruit. Disconnect from electricity prior to removing hopper in event of a jam. Ensure learners are fully trained and supervised in mill operation.	No
Press use injury – press arm may fall when cheeses are being loaded.	Learners, tutor.	Ensure press arm is held by someone whilst press is being loaded. Ensure all learners communicate clearly to ensure press is clear before lowering press arm.	No

Action required to Reduce Risk | By Whom
See above actions proposed to reduce risk. | Tutor
Person carrying out Risk Assessment | **Lorraine Turnbull, Tutor**
Date of Assessment | **19/04/2016**
Review date | **19/10/2016**
Risk Assessment level: Negligible/Slight.

Other Requirements

If you host outdoor courses at your own premises you will need public liability insurance, adequate toilet facilities, and a designated first-aider with first aid box and accident book. Indoors you will also need a fire-safety plan with exits marked, working fire extinguishers, adequate heating and ventilation, possibly a classroom with tables and chairs, a projector and screen, and probably a laptop. Workshop teaching such as the welding and blacksmithing courses John taught, require additional technical and safety rules and storage. You don't need a food hygiene certificate to offer your learners tea and biscuits, and they can bring their own packed lunch.

Disabled Access

Making proper provision for learners with disabilities is not without its challenges. The public institutions I used to work for were asked from time to time to enrol learners with disabilities. Naturally they wanted to be seen to be providing learning for all, and indeed, under the 2010 Equality Act they have a duty to do so. In practice, reconciling the physical demands of a subject, the additional support necessary to meet the needs of students with disabilities, with the learning experience of other students sometimes proved impossible.

I was once asked to include a wheelchair user on a farm-based practical lambing workshop. To accommodate this learner alongside the others would have been very difficult: we would have had to cut the group size to allow everyone their hands-on experience, and also to have had at least one learning support assistant in attendance which meant the course would have run at a loss. I would have had to write a bespoke risk assessment to cover additional hazards; including contamination of the wheelchair, access, safe handling, and lifting; but it was the prospect of trying to manoeuvre both a ewe in labour and the wheelchair to allow full participation that proved to be the insurmountable hurdle. Sadly it was decided that we couldn't accommodate this particular learner's needs.

Structuring classes and courses

Learners are happiest in a relaxed and friendly atmosphere. In an old-style classroom you can help create this by arranging the seats in a circle, rather than rows, remembering to put visual aids such as flipcharts, whiteboard, and screen where everyone can see them. A friendly greeting and a cup of tea or coffee is a good start, and an update on house rules such as the smoking policy, breaks, location of toilets and so on, will help put everyone at their ease.

Before you launch into the lesson proper, find out how much your learners already know via a general discussion. This breaks the ice as well as helping you weigh up the new intake. For instance, if I were running a pruning workshop I'd ask how many people had their own apple trees, and how many had previously done any pruning at all. The discussion would usually progress from there as the learners start to contribute. I would then write two or three aims or objectives (basically a summary of what I intend to cover) on a whiteboard which I would revisit at the end of the day.

Anyone planning to deliver a speech or a lesson or practical demonstration will need some sort of notes, whether prompt-cards or a full-blown lesson plan. For one-day workshops I usually wrote a single side of A4, but for a course of six lessons I would produce a lesson plan for each day and a session plan to cover the whole course. This allowed me a bit of latitude to alter and move the lessons around according to factors such as the weather or the group's progress. A lesson plan is a flexible document and should be used as such. If after the end of a lesson you felt that a particular activity or part of the lesson didn't get the results you hoped for, then examine it and amend the plan. Did you run out of time? Was the activity too easy or too complex? Make changes and review the plan. It might take a couple of lessons to iron out timings of activities. Sometimes if things are going wrong having another teacher sit in and see through fresh eyes can identify and resolve the problem.

Running through what you plan to cover in a lesson or workshop is very important and becomes easier as you gain experience. Taking the example of the one-day apple juicing workshop as detailed in the risk assessment, you might think that it only needs an afternoon. But when you start to break down the activities and combine theoretical classroom-based learning with the practical activity, you can see that it really needs a full six-hour workshop. You also need to factor in tea, lunch or comfort breaks, which can become more of a problem when teaching outdoor subjects in winter, such as tree pruning or lambing; and of course you have to leave enough time for Q&A.

Breaking a lesson down into short periods allows you to divide it with breaks or to change your delivery style. It's a long day if you have a three-hour slot in the morning for a PowerPoint presentation. I liked to start with a gentle introduction, possibly accompanied by tea and biscuits, so a relevant film clip (YouTube offers a wealth of material, or you can prepare your own) or a short slot with props may be a good way to break the ice. I also like to follow an intensive session, where perhaps I've introduced some maths or scientific vocabulary, with something completely different.

Adult learners are sometimes resistant to working in pairs or groups, so to get round it I have occasionally tried splitting the group in two. This worked well if I introduced an element of competition, such as having a mini-quiz at the end of the day. By this time, the learners have got to know each other and have relaxed.

Praise plays a vital part here: some learners have difficulty socialising with complete strangers: they might feel anxious that they don't know as much as everybody else, or they might just be shy about contributing in a group. Lots of encouragement and praise will help them to join in.

Allowing time for students to share their thoughts with you allows you to assess their progress, revisit things they didn't understand or felt difficult, or explain things in a different way. Remind hesitant learners of the progress they've made since arriving that morning. If it's a one-day workshop, offer information on how they can progress further learning be it via YouTube, the internet, or courses available elsewhere. At the end of the course remember to thank your attendees. At this time, perhaps sending them off with a paper *aide memoire* of the other courses you offer might be appropriate.

I've detailed a basic lesson plan below, but you can simplify or add to it as best suits your requirements.

Session Plan – Juicing workshop   Tutor – Lorraine Turnbull   10am -1pm, 1.30pm-4.30pm   Spotty Dog Cider

AIMS: To enable learners to confidently begin to make apple juice and craft cider

OBJECTIVES: All learners will operate juicing machinery safely, most learners will identify apple types, all learners will list necessary equipment and process.

TIMING	CONTENT	LEARNER ACTIVITIES	RESOURCES	ASSESSMENT
10.00-10.30	Introduction, review of aims & objectives of workshop.	Recognise own personal objectives, ascertain own prior experience in subject.	Register, risk assessment, information sheet, initial assessment discussion	Discussion to identify level of learning – self assessment by learner, assessment by tutor.
10.30-11.15	Apple varieties & characteristics – what they impart to juice & cider.	Identify different types of apple – desert, culinary & cider.	PP presentation Samples of apples for tasting.	Group discussion followed by individual Q&A on tastes.
11.15-12.00	equipment & process	Examine equipment, follow flowchart, group discussion. Learn Food safety information	Equipment, flowchart, pH paper, hydrometer Handout.	Contribute to group discussion, individual Q&A to identify equipment and order of flowchart
1200-13.00	Making cider – fermentation & maturation	Demonstrate use of hydrometer, pH readings.	Hydrometer, pH paper, cider	By demonstration and Q&A.
13.30-1430	Storage & pasteurisation	Visit maturation shed, watch pasteurisation process. Reference handout.	Cider, pasteurisers, thermometer, handout.	Discussion and Q&A session.
14.30- 1600	Practical Juice session.	Learners to wash, pulp & press own juice, using equipment.	Apples, pulper, press, containers.	By individual Q&A, by demonstration
16.00-16.30	Plenary, housekeeping	Learners to consolidate learning by asking questions, annotate handouts. Feedback to tutor.	Handout, tutor feedback sheet.	By personal feedback session, group feedback, further information etc.

Charging

When you are putting together your own courses you need to think carefully about your prices. Factors that help determine them might be geographical (you will have a larger catchment if you are near a town or city); popularity (there are always people who want to go on basic courses such as chicken keeping or bee keeping); and rarity (courses such as blacksmithing are not as common and therefore command a higher price). Overheads affecting the price are insurance, advertising, utilities, stationery, and raw materials. The gross profit should reflect the value of your stock in trade, which happens to be your time and expertise.

A basic rate of £14 an hour must surely be your minimum, so for a six-hour practical workshop such as the juicing one, I'd be looking at a maximum of six learners at £30 each, yielding £180 for the day – enough to cover my expenses and pay me a decent wage, but not high enough to be off-putting to the customer. If I'm inundated with applicants then I can raise my price to say £35 a head. If you are uncomfortable about pricing simply check what your competitors are charging, and what the customer gets for it. For a beekeeping experience, I used to limit the number to three: four people around a single hive was manageable, and out of the £40 a head I charged, I could afford to buy bee-suits for my learners.

In a classroom-based presentation with no practical session, I usually limited the class size to 12. I kept advertising costs down by using social media and local radio, which was often free, and putting up posters locally. The best day for classes, I found, was Saturday; midweek courses had to be fitted round work and school commitments, and Sunday was regarded by most candidates as a family day. I avoided the school holidays altogether. Make sure your terms and conditions (especially regarding cancellation!) are printed in full on any printed or on-line brochures, and booking forms, and ensure that candidates tick the "I have read the T&C" box, and send an email acknowledgement on receipt of payment.

TOP TIPS FOR SUCCESS

- Make it interesting
- Make it age/ability appropriate
- Use a mix of learning styles
- How are you going to measure learning?
- Use a lesson plan however informal

CASE STUDY –
Dardarroch Farm

Erica Wallbank
Dardarroch Farm
Galloway
Scotland
www.thewomanthatfarms.co.uk
Facebook.com/thewomanthatfarms

Erica moved to her first 3 acre smallholding in 2003 with her two young children and two dogs. With no prior knowledge, she took the plunge to fulfil a lifelong dream and has never looked back! Moving into the old farmhouse in mid-winter meant she had to learn quickly. She then cleared old farm buildings ready for spring and livestock.

Working 10 miles way from her smallholding was difficult, and Erica soon set up a home-based business. The rare breed poultry and ducks began to produce more eggs than the family could consume, and in various ways they started to more than pay for themselves. The small poultry hobby took off and developed into a fully-fledged business. After just 3 months Erica quit her job and became a full-time smallholder! To supplement this, she also started buying at car boot sales and selling via an internet auction site. This all helped to provide Erica with the means to continue her smallholding lifestyle.

Erica now owns a 40 acre organic smallholding in Scotland, where she lives with a mixed herd of

Dexter and Limousin cattle, Ryeland and Texel sheep, pigs, goats and poultry. She grows cut flowers and fruit and vegetables for her family and the B&B, tearoom & restaurant she runs, and also has an on-farm shop. Erica also offers some courses in a wide range of subjects. This year she is increasing growing areas and adding glasshouses, and aiming to make these productive.

Top Tip – There are many reasons I chose this lifestyle – a deep love and respect for nature, animals and the land, being self-sufficient and being able to feed my family the best quality food I can provide. But also, to leave a legacy for my children. However, this doesn't mean you have to be poor! If I kept the holding as it is and developed slowly I'd say I'd get about £20,000 year from my 40 acre farm. If you want the lifestyle and to have money it is possible if you are prepared to put in the work and effort, I'm living testament to that. Someone once said to me – "Erica, You can't have it all." My reply was "Why not?"

Chapter 9
Promoting your Business

Working hard to produce goods on your smallholding or creating courses for people to fill is not by itself going to sell anything. You need a marketplace, customers and an attractive sales pitch. Whether your market is local, national or even international, whether it's a physical place or an online store, YOU need to make your customers aware you exist, and create a method of telling them how to contact you and how to buy from you.

Every smallholding and rural business is different, as are the people who run them, and different products and services lend themselves to different kinds of marketing. Variety makes the world go round, and we each of us have preferences and dislikes. Let's assume you have a product to sell. It's a great product; now, how are you going to sell it?

Well, different products and different services need different approaches to sales; I think we would all agree. I probably wouldn't buy shoes online, but prefer to visit a shoe shop and look, feel and try on different pairs before buying, but I'm happy to go online to purchase a book or DVD. If we divide "things for sale" into services and products, this may be a good place to start. In the main, services include holiday lets, evening classes or courses, jobs carried out by tradesmen (plumbing etc), book-keeping, web-design etc.

The definition has been blurred lately, as lots of educational courses are now strictly on-line learning experiences, but I think you get the general idea. Products are those tangible items that you can buy, whether this is from shops, farmers markets, online or direct from the farm. A jar of honey is a product, a leather belt is a product, a tractor is a product, but bee-keeping is a service, leather-making is a trade or service, and farming is a service.

Whether your customer buys over the telephone, internet or in person, you need to ensure he or she knows you exist and where, how to get in touch and how they can spend their money buying your stuff! The Covid-19 pandemic has forced many retailers to think outside the box and café owners now offer take-away meals and sandwiches, cider producers offer small pouches of cider for off the premises consumption, and home delivery, so be inventive to stay ahead of the game.

Markets

Traditionally, many smallholders, farms and food producers made a significant proportion of sales at farmers markets or food fairs where you get to keep the entire profit net of stall rent. The smaller country produce markets generally held in church halls and run by volunteers are unlikely to sell enough to make the ordeal worth it: I tried the nearest such market when I was selling eggs, honey and plants. It was boring and stuffy and not the kind of marketplace my aspiring foodies frequented. I never made enough to cover my time and I lasted eight weeks. I'd never recommend them, unless they significantly update themselves. Ordinary weekly town markets are also probably not much use to the artisan producers: the majority of stalls are straightforward price cutters, and the clientele are only after mainstream products at rock-bottom prices.

Farmers markets and food or craft fairs are the way to go. They are more vibrant and dynamic. The clientele is more affluent and more sophisticated and has come to taste and shop. Farmers markets also routinely sell alcohol, which most others don't. (Remember, though, that if you want to sell your cider or mead or fruit liqueur at a market you need to check well in advance whether it has a liquor licence. If not, you have 10 working days to apply for a Temporary Events Notice). Try and ensure you have regular days at markets if possible. Your loyal customers want to know you are always there on a Thursday and may make a special trip just to buy from you. When I sold cider at Padstow Food Fair I tried to book every Friday, Saturday and Sunday in the holiday season. Some markets are better-attended than others, so before you commit, pay a visit and talk to one or two of the stallholders. Find your nearest farmers market(s) on the National Farmers' Retail & Markets Association website **www.farma.org.uk**.

A much more recent development is The Food Assembly, a social enterprise, originally set up in France but now spreading all over Europe, to bring customers and local producers together. Customers place their orders online and every week meet the producers at a local venue to collect their orders and socialise. Customers get better food, and you, the producer, get a fair price: you set your own price and keep 80% of it. The rest is divided between the local Assembly organisers and the venue. This compares to the 15-25% of the sale price most supermarkets will pay you, so if you're looking for a new sales platform the Food Assembly is well worth considering. For more details visit **www.foodassembly.com**.

In the market itself, even more so than at your own premises, presentation is every bit as important as the goods on display. Your stall will be signed using the same fonts and colours as the signs back at the holding (and I'll say more about branding shortly). Shoppers shop with their senses. They are visually attracted to colourful and interesting stalls. They may also follow the smell of the food or other products on offer. Most will stop in front of your stall to browse. Attractive packaging, clear prices and a friendly and knowledgeable salesperson are important. If you are selling food, a clean apron and neat, tidy hair will inspire confidence. Little samples of food or drink will often result in sales. A simple A5 sheet or brochure with your prices, contact details and order form should be popped into the bag with customers' purchases and also handed out off-stall to generate repeat business. (If yours is a visitor-friendly holding, copies of the same brochure can be left in pubs, cafes, hotel and B&B foyers, the TIC (Tourist Information Centre) and elsewhere to direct visitors from outside the district to your premises).

As a footnote, it's definitely worth selling fresh, seasonal produce at an attended roadside stall (preferably fronted by a safe and convenient lay-by or forecourt!). As with the market, you get the full retail price but you don't even have to pay a stall fee. And if you don't already have and don't want to invest in an open-fronted shed for the purpose, you can even use your actual market stall. But this kind of stall is more than just a generator of cash: its actual takings may not be great, but it makes great public relations. Even passing motorists who have no intention of stopping to buy will notice you, maybe for future reference, maybe not. The point is that every single person in the district will know who and where you are; and if you have something a bit out of the mainstream to offer – you might have a tree or two of russets, or a vast range of red-hot chillies, for example – people will be tempted.

Signage

Perhaps the most obvious, and yet most important consideration for even the smallest of rural businesses is signage, because if people can't find you your products are going to sit on the shelf. And a tatty hand-painted board doesn't inspire confidence. Well-made directional signage in a large, clear font will bring customers to your gate; the sign at your entrance should be visible from some distance away to give drivers time to register and should carry your opening hours, phone number, and web and email addresses. One thing to beware of is that signage is tightly controlled by planning regulations: you may need permission even to put a sign up at your own front gate, and if you want a brown tourism sign you will have to pay the local authority's Highways Department a fortune for the privilege. All signs should be consistent with your branding, of which more below.

Business Name

The name you pick for your business is all part of the marketing, and once you've chosen it you're stuck with it, so spend a lot of time thinking about it. In many cases the name will be a simple descriptor of where you are and what you do: Calder Valley Holiday Cottages or Axminster Mead leave no-one in any doubt, and make internet searches very easy. But christening a business that does many different things, such as a smallholding selling hay, organic vegetables, and home-produced beef and pork, as well as contracting services, is trickier. Perhaps just leave it at the name of the farm? Or combine the name of the farm with a brief description such as Smith's Traditional Meats or Smith's Independent Farm Shop?

The internet has an important part in choosing a name, too.

One way of helping internet customers search for you might be to include your town or county in the domain name. Any search for a holiday cottage in the Calder Valley or mead in Devon will come to your site straight away. Check whether your preferred domain name (the wording of your website address) and email address are already taken before you do anything else: if they're not available you'll have to rethink all the branding you were planning for labels, letterheads, the design of your market stall, signage – the lot.

And make your domain name short – it'll be much more memorable. I'm more likely to remember Spotty Dog Cider than North Cornwall Artisan Cider Barn.

Business Name Tips

- Choose a suitable name, easy to spell and remember
- Check with Companies House that no-one is already using it
- Check the domain name is available
- Check social media page/names are also available

Branding

Picking a memorable name and having a consistent theme running throughout your design are important, and if you're in doubt there are plenty of companies that specialise in getting your marketing right. But they'll charge, so before you pay for domain names, social media names, getting a website up and running and so on, think long and hard about branding.

Branding is basically design. Good branding makes your product or service stand out and should be easy to remember, to recognise, and most important of all, to identify with. Who are your target customers? Are they male or female? What age bracket are they in? Are they locals or tourists? What are their interests? By thinking about how they think, you should be able to create branding to appeal to them.

When I started to look at branding my cider, I decided to aim for the contemporary artisan cider lover and to keep my marketing and sales local to North Cornwall, where it was a "well-kept secret" produced only in small batches from local apples. It was a great success and basically sold itself at farmers markets and food fairs.

I approached a linocut artist whose work I admired to design a logo I would use on my website, my bottle labels, and all advertising to promote a brand image. The Spotty Dog logo was based on my blue-roan Cocker spaniel and was executed in black and white (cheap to print and stunningly simple). It appealed to both traditional and contemporary markets and could be easily adapted as a label design as more varieties of cider were developed, for example, a batch of cider called Seadog utilised the original Spotty Dog head with the addition of a pirate hat with a red ribbon on it. Again, simple and cheap to print but visually attractive. The name Seadog was attractive to customers as we were based on the North coast of Cornwall and sold our cider to local pubs and at local produce markets, and we rapidly sold out.

The Internet

The internet is now the first place most people look these days when searching for any product or service, so the right presence is of critical importance. It's also a good idea to sell as much as you can online and directly, so you don't have to share the profit with a third-party retailer. And it all starts with a website.

Website

A website is essential to many businesses, and it has to be a good one. It should go without saying that your website needs to include every relevant fact about who you are, where you are, what you do, and how to get in touch with you – and include it prominently and plainly. If the site carries any material that dates it, it should be updated assiduously and frequently – you shouldn't be announcing a special offer on alpaca wool blankets that expired three weeks ago. If there's anything interactive on it – in particular, an order-form and payment details – make sure it's very, very easy to navigate. The overall design should be very carefully chosen to carry your branding – fonts, colours, logos, borders, every last detail – and to appeal strongly to your chosen demographic: it's no good some whiz-kid designer embellishing the site with lasers and glitter-balls if your range is mainly composed of hand-turned walking sticks and briar pipes. Use lots of appealing and appropriate pictures.

None of this is free. You have to rent a domain name, pay a company to host your site, and more often than not, unless you have a background in design, hire a web-designer. But it's not optional. It's both your shop window and your shop. If it's done badly it's a complete waste of money. If it's done properly it will repay your investment over and over again.

When someone searches for your product, your website should appear at or near the top of the list. This means Search Engine Optimisation. Websites compete for attention and ranking in the search engines and people with the knowledge to use SEO will benefit from increased traffic and visibility. But it's complicated and, as with all things computer-related, you can get so bound up in it that you start neglecting the real business of growing and making things.

Search Engine Optimisation is a process used by businesses

to increase their presence when being searched through internet search engines. Websites compete for attention and ranking in the search engines and those who have the knowledge can use SEO to benefit from increased traffic and visibility.

When someone uses a search engine the results are displayed according to relevance and authority. Authority is mainly decided by the number and quality of links (known as backlinks) from other web pages. Ultimately, SEO has become much more sophisticated since its inception; however, it's still about keywords and links, and the relevance, reputation and quality of them. It's also about quality of content (keyword rich, unique and relative to the page's meta data) and visitor satisfaction. A good user experience, meaning the searcher has clicked through and visited for longer than say a few seconds, is noted by the search engine analytics and is key to success.

How fast your site loads up, and whether you have a responsive site, is becoming increasingly important when looking at how high you can go in the ratings. A responsive site is built on a framework that stacks the content and re-adjusts the size of the text and imagery making it simple to navigate and read via a smaller screen or mobile device. For some further information on appropriate use of heading tags visit **http://yoast.com/headings-use/**

If you have any means of eliciting information from your website visitors, either via an email contact or a shopping cart, you must add a GDPR and cookie policy notice to your website. This is now a legal requirement. I have summarised mine here for my holiday letting business in France, but it's easy to adapt.

GDPR, Cookie & Privacy Policy

The European regulation No. 2016/679 of 27 April 2016, or General Data Protection Regulation (GDPR), came into force on 25 May 2018. Basically this replaces the Data Protection Act. This is a European-wide law and as such affects how we use and store information we receive from guests and enquirers. It covers all data, whether electronic or paper based.

We use cookies on our website. Cookies are text files placed on your computer to collect standard internet log information and visitor behaviour information. This information is used to track visitors' use of the website and to compile statistical reports on website activity. You can set your browser not to accept cookies. See **www.aboutcookies.org** for more information).

What information we collect from you.

When you make a booking with us we collect the names of all the guests who will be staying, the home address, email address and telephone number of the person making the booking.

How we use the information you give us

We use your email to communicate with you, to send you booking confirmation and answer any queries you email us, and to thank you after your visit and ask you for a review.

Marketing

We now send occasional marketing newsletters. You have to actively subscribe to these and can unsubscribe at any time. We never pass your details to any third party.

Access to your Information

You have the right to request a copy of the information we hold about you. If you would like a copy of this please email us at **xxxxxxxx@gmail.com**

Right to be Forgotten

All customers have the right to ask us to remove their details from our records. We are also required by law to keep financial records for 7 years, so guests cannot ask to be erased from these financial records.

Be assured that your details are kept secure on our system via password-controlled entry and are not used for any other purpose or shared with any other person or business. Similarly, if you choose to follow us on social media we don't need consent as you have already accepted the terms & conditions on that platform.

Notification of Data Breaches

The GDPR will require us to notify the Information Commissioner's Office within 72 hours of first having become aware of the breach where that breach is likely to "result in a risk for the rights and freedoms of individuals". For any breach, we are required to notify the customers "without undue delay" after first becoming aware of a data breach.

Online Shopping Cart

Most websites now have the facility to add in an online shopping cart, where customers can collect goods, add them to their shopping trolleys and pay securely for them. Most web designers can set this up for you quickly. If you don't have a website yet, or don't have enough products to justify a trolley option, you can always offer payment by paypal, which just requires a valid email address. You just have to organise the delivery. The customer is there, looking at the merchandise online on your shop. Just one click and he's bought! What are you waiting for?

Email Newsletters

Encourage and reward your loyal customers by collecting their email addresses and setting up a newsletter with plenty of exclusive deals and discounts. Exclusivity is something that people will pay for! Keep your mailing list up to date but make sure you have the recipient's explicit permission to send them newsletters; this means having a "tick the box" section on your newsletter sign-up form. Try to have at least a quarterly newsletter, and short and sweet is better than nothing at all. Tell them about the new offers you have, how lambing went this year, about the owl family that has appeared in the orchard. It's not just an occasion to hard-sell; take the time to communicate to them. Directing them to a new video on the website will get them back to your website and shop. Mailchimp and Mailerlite are just two apps available.

Social Media

It can take a while to get comfortable with social media if you are new to it, but it's worth it. Different social media platforms – Facebook, Twitter, Instagram and so forth – have different demographics, so match your platform to the audience you're trying to reach. Include lots of links to your website (and vice versa). Lack of social media presence invites your younger customers to question you. A business with a social media presence is automatically viewed as more professional these days. An active presence is even better, so post as regularly as you can, and at least weekly. To make it more effective:

- Use pictures. Facebook posts with images win twice as much engagement as those without; on Twitter the figure is 150%.
- Make it real: don't "sell" all the time. Engage with your potential customers warmly and cheerfully.
- Respond to comments and questions as soon as possible. Politely!
- Keep an eye on the analytics. Facebook insights are free. Instagram and Twitter also have analytics tools. Check your posts to see which perform best.
- Avoid personal or political statements. It's a business page. Your customers don't want to know.

If you're unsure about content, look at your competitors. If you're a cidermaker talk about the great harvest (with photos of ripe fruit), or your upcoming Wassail (with more details on our website to attract people), or that award you won. To save yourself effort, link your website to your Facebook or Twitter account and just post once.

Facebook

This is a great place to start. It has more than a billion daily users, including a sizeable proportion of middle-aged and older people who don't use other platforms as much. You have to register as an individual before you can add a business page.

Have a compact and informative 'about' section to describe your business. It's all about personality, so think about the kind of customers you want to attract and use the photographs and 'about' section to appeal to them. You need to speak, act and think like your target audience. An introductory video could be just the tool to catch people's attention. Keep it short, to the point and a showcase for your business. If a picture is worth a thousand words, then a video is worth ten thousand. They want to see 'behind the scenes' photos, they want to see special offers, any awards you've won, product demonstrations, celebrity endorsements, contests and competitions. Consistency in what you post on social media, your website and your blog is important. Check your facts, prices, opening times etc for inaccuracies.

- Choose your profile picture and cover photo with great care: they need to be clear, sharp, and relevant.
- Have a compact and informative 'about' section to describe your business. It's all about personality, so think about the kind of customers you want to attract and try to speak, act and think like your target audience.
- Check the insights tab to see who is viewing your posts. Not getting the response you want? Then perhaps try a different approach. And remember to check the analytics after a few days.

Instagram

This is a much more visual medium, great for products that lend themselves to arresting imagery: glasses of sparkling cider, trees just dripping with ripe apples...you get the idea. It's the fastest growing platform, and used mainly by younger audiences. They want eye-catching instant images and this tool suits them. My website and social media pages included lots of photographs of my orchard, the trees, fruit and the cider making process. I also included lots of photos of wildlife. It's not just the cider that people want to buy; it's the lifestyle. Hashtags are a way to labelling your content with keywords so it is more likely to be seen. The trick is to use the right hashtags. Search 'hashtags for Instagram' or 'Websta' for pointers.

Twitter

I've only recently started to use this and it's very fast-paced, so you need to post several times a day, even every half an hour, to make sure your tweets don't get lost in the noise. There is a huge audience available, but it can be a serious drain on your time.

Internet training

If you've read this far and feel overwhelmed by the vocabulary, or fear that you don't have the technical ability to embrace social media, get some training. I attended a four-day "build your own website" course using Wordpress. For the first day I was totally out of my depth and drove home with a massive headache. But the next day was better, and although I was slower than most of the other whiz-kids on the course I could see my website taking shape and my confidence started to grow. A few months later, I returned to the centre to learn about social media and how it could help my business. At the time I didn't really know what Facebook was, but within a few weeks, I was posting simultaneously on Facebook and on my website, and yes, my sales were increasing. My advice would be to go on a course if you can, read tutorials and watch videos on the internet and *try* it.

The internet is the future and if you want to succeed in business you need o at least have a website and the knowledge to use it. Take it one step at a time, and open yourself up to a whole new world out there.

Couriers

Now, if you sell goods online and have to use a parcel delivery service or courier, ensure you do your homework. Customer Service is key, and sadly poor packaging or courier services come up really high on the list of complaints of poor customer service. So, pay a little extra for a company with a good record, and spend a little more on protective packaging. Remember, you want to keep regular customers, not spend all your time trying to find new ones.

Finally, my website and social media pages include many photographs of my orchard, the trees, fruit and the cider making process. I also include lots of photos of wildlife. A marketing event I attended a few years ago was enlightening. I realised that it wasn't just the cider that people wanted to buy; it was the lifestyle! People were yearning for a simpler way of life, with golden days in the orchard and bees buzzing softly in the blossom. By thinking about what your customer actually wants, you can help yourself to marketing your product properly. Photographs of dirty farmyards are not going to do your product any favours! Poor, handmade signage to your farm shop is NOT inviting – it looks amateurish and unprofessional. And badly trained and untidy staff will result in poor feedback and customers talking about you for all the wrong reasons. Make it interesting, make it fun, and make it aspirational.

CASE STUDY –
Leadketty Farm

Harold, Moira & Stephen Corrigall
Leadketty Farm
Perthshire
www.leadkettyfarm.co.uk
FB: www.facebook.com/leadkettyfarm/

Leadketty Farm is a smallholding in all but name. The 12 hectare (30 acre) holding is located in the centre of the main berry growing region of Eastern Scotland. The Corrigalls have farmed for eighty years, and switched from cultivating potatoes to soft fruit many years ago. They now cultivate 27 acres of strawberries in grow-bags filled with coconut husk, on irrigated table-tops under polytunnels and 3 acres of raspberries, producing an average of 350 tonnes of fruit annually.

Thanks to innovations of protected cropping and production of earlier and later varieties, the UK strawberry season now runs for 20 weeks. Polytunnels offer protection from wind, rain and many pests and diseases. Pollination inside the tunnels is provided by mobile mini-hives of bumblebees, who are more efficient pollinators than honeybees, with no desire to migrate. A mobile hive contains around 100 workers and will pollinate for 6-8 weeks.

The majority of their produce is supplied to UK supermarkets through a cooperative. The Corrigalls have embraced the Red Tractor Marketing Scheme, and also offer around 10% of their fruit to local hotels, shops and businesses. As a mainly seasonal producer, 75 seasonal (mainly migrant) staff are employed from May through till October, and are housed on-site in residential caravans and are charged for accommodation and electricity. The situation with Brexit is high on their concerns for future employment.

Smallholders have found an increased demand from supermarkets, jam producers and smaller food businesses. Strawberries and raspberries are the main crops, with increasing demand for blueberries, gooseberries and blackcurrants.

Quote – "We do not know if we will manage to continue if there was any increase on the living wage, e.g. overtime or the six monthly increase, then there is no way we feel our business would be viable. If Scotland lost the fruit industry it would be a huge blow to the economy and that is what's at stake." – Harold Corrigall

Chapter 10
Sustainability & Self sufficiency

Sustainability and self-sufficiency isn't just about saving the planet, fantastic and topical though it may be. It's about adopting a lifestyle or running a business that does not devour precious resources, be they money, water or electricity, and without diminishing the natural environment. On a simple scale, this can start to be achieved by just making some simple lifestyle changes, such as recycling and switching off lights when they are not required, but changing your mindset to really embrace a better way of life needn't be difficult if you try and make one big change every few months. It may be hip to be sustainable right now, but if it makes your life more efficient and saves money too, then shouldn't you be prepared to read this chapter and see what changes you could make, and the money you could save?

Top 5 Quick Sustainable Changes

1. Install flush reducers

Home-made flush reducers can be made from a plastic 1or 1.5 litre drinks bottle, filled with sand or small pebbles, topped with water and screwed tight, and then placed inside the WC cistern. This can reduce the amount of water reduced per flush considerably (a normal toilet takes 9 litres to flush). That's quite a saving even from one toilet annually. If you have a modern 2 flush button on your WC, you don't have to do this.

2. Use non-plastic teabags

At the end of 2019, over 90% of teabags used in the UK contained non-biodegradable polypropylene. This can't be composted, so switch to a plastic-free teabag, such as those made by Clipper, PG Tips and Pukka. Many tea producers are in the process of switching to plastic free.

3. Compost green and brown waste

Loads of councils are charging by weight for domestic rubbish. Recycle your veg peelings, plastic free teabags, grass cuttings and autumn leaves to make compost for your garden. Don't include dairy, meat, fish or cooked food remains.

4. Stop buying bottled water

If you must have a bottle of water, reuse one, fill from the tap, use a water filter and keep in the fridge.

5. Stop using fabric conditioner

It's full of silicon and can be easily replaced with a capful of white vinegar. This will prevent residue and smells in your washing machine, and make your towels fluffier and more absorbent.

The UK has a long way to go to make mainstream farming more sustainable, but things are changing. Defra acknowledges in its *Strategy for Sustainable Farming & Food* that British agriculture has somewhat failed to perform economically, environmentally and socially. Farm profitability is at its lowest since the 1930s, and agriculture gobbles up something like £25bn a year of taxpayers' money in direct subsidies (a mere £3bn), grants, and exemptions from business rates, fuel duty, VAT, corporation tax, and inheritance tax.

In early 2020 British farms, unable to secure seasonal migrant workers from the EU due to combination of Brexit and Covid-19 restrictions, actively asked for furloughed and unemployed workers and students to help out by working on British farms. There was a muted response, and the situation and future ramifications are causing alarm in the farming and horticultural sectors, and in Westminster.

On a positive note, we now have an increased understanding of sustainability in farming and processing that reduces both waste and cost. And we know that we can all, both as individuals and as businesses, make small changes that together add up to huge differences. The smallholding and small rural business sector is possibly at the forefront of demonstrating sustainable practices, and aspiring and existing small businesses in the land-based sector are urged to continue to develop sustainability wherever possible.

When John and I moved to our neglected little bungalow in Cornwall it was in a bit of a sorry state. It was basically a building sitting inside an acre of paddock, with no fencing and a large dilapidated shed. As far as self-sufficiency was concerned it was a blank canvas. Our first job was to install central heating, as the house had only electric storage heaters (none of which worked) and a warped, draughty wood burner. We decided straightaway to install two independent heating systems: a solid fuel system to use up the large supply of cheap or free timber we could access, and an LPG system with combi-boiler for very cold days (like many rural properties there was no mains gas supply).

John, who has experience of plumbing, crawled around under the floor, fitting pipes for both systems and then we arranged professionals to connect one set of pipes to the woodburner, and the other set to the LPG boiler. The donkey work done by John saved us a huge amount of money, and whilst he was moving around under the floor he lined in between the joists with insulation panels cut to fit, reducing the drafts and instantly making the house more efficient at retaining heat. The bedrooms each had two radiators, one fed by the LPG and one from the woodburner, as did the bathroom, and the bath and kitchen sink had one extra tap connected to the back-boiler from the woodburner. The defunct storage heaters were removed, and the old woodburner was removed for later installation in the large shed, which we later used for hosting courses. The cost of installing two systems was recouped within 18 months, so well worth the investment.

In the second year, we removed all the old and meagre roof insulation and as part of a government scheme paid £1 to have new insulation installed. Now this was a few years ago, but there are still incentives out there to make your home more efficient, so have a look at **www.simpleenergyadvice.org. uk/pages/green-homes-grant**. The old insulation wasn't wasted either; we took the plastic panel off the bath and stuffed the void around the bath with it, keeping bathwater hotter for longer, and stuffed the rest inside panelling inside the shed to insulate it too. We also had cavity wall insulation installed, and new double glazing to replace the windows where the seals had broken down, and soon the house was warm and cosy, and the central heating was used only for heating water, and in very cold temperatures to heat the house. We estimated that our fuel bills dropped considerably, and we saved £700 per year on the cost of LPG, burned 2 tonne less of wood annually in the woodburner, and our electricity bills also dropped.

Talking about woodburners, did you know that candle-ends and pine cones make great firelighters? Pine cones are particularly good options as they are very sustainable, and a bracing walk through pine woods can fill an old feed-sack with enough pine cones to last a good few weeks.

Light bulbs are another easy-to-change thing you can do. In our smallholding in Cornwall, we changed all the light bulbs to energy saving ones inside the house, and replaced the outdoor floodlights and security lights too, from 150 Watt halogen bulbs to 9 Watt LEDs which we fitted with PIRs. We had three outside lights, so reduced the total usage from 450 Watts to 27 Watts. You just need to go round your farm or smallholding and count all the outdoor lights you have to see the savings you could make! When we moved to France our house had many energy saving light bulbs and many ceiling-fitted spotlights, with halogen 50 Watt bulbs in the kitchen and in both our gites, and the bathroom fitted vanity units were burning 20 Watt halogen bulbs in them. So, the vanity unit bulbs were changed to 1.5 Watt LEDs and the ceiling spots changed to 3.5 Watt LEDs. Electricity is very expensive in France, so we knew we would be saving a considerable sum just doing this. We chose warm white bulbs, which are a more natural light than cool white.

In time, we adopted other tiny ideas to help us save money, as they occurred, or as we could afford. Painting the walls and ceilings white and positioning large mirrors to reflect daylight coming in the windows meant we didn't need lights on even on gloomy winter days, and at night the rooms seem to be brighter.

As we were both working from home, we downsized to one vehicle. We saved on insurance, maintenance costs and fuel, and the vehicle was large enough to pull our livestock trailer in case we needed capacity for animals or other bulky or heavy items.

Using a pressure cooker to make large batches of soups or stews quickly and using very little electricity or gas and then filling clean, used food containers, such as old ice-cream tubs, is a great use of time and will quickly fill your freezer with lots of home-produced ready-meals. Recycled, clean plastic milk containers can be used to fill with apple or fruit juice and frozen, or used to create chicken water troughs. Cut a window on the long side of the container to allow birds to access clean water. If they become dirty or damaged you can simply recycle them in your recycling domestic waste.

As we started to meet other smallholders, we were introduced to further innovations, many of which we shamelessly stole for our own use. The tumble drier was sold as we had no use for it once John rigged up a clothes airer above the woodburner, and a washing line inside the polytunnel.

The large dilapidated shed had the walls lined with chipboard and the small gap stuffed, as mentioned before, with the old loft insulation. Strip lights were replaced with some LED lights, and a few of the concrete roofing panels replaced with clear ones to allow us to work during the day without artificial light. The old woodburner was installed in this shed, and an old large table we collected after seeing it on Freecycle was given centre space in the shed. This is where I spent many a long day labelling bottles of cider, teaching courses, and where John would sit with small items of machinery requiring servicing or repair.

We recycled rainwater in IBC containers strategically placed both around the outside of the house and the shed, which was used to water the polytunnel and for washing the car and yard down after cider production. Here in France, IBCs are worth their weight in gold, but with droughts every summer, we really needed to increase our rainwater harvesting capacity to allow regular watering of our potagers and the apple orchard. With the right filtering, we could even divert surplus water into the swimming pool; after all, it is thereafter chemically treated and filtered to be safe.

Soon we were routinely practicing the 3Rs – reduce, reuse, and recycle – without really even being aware of it. I'm happy to share some ideas here with you, in the hope that you consider and even try some out and see what savings you can make.

Old gutters can be reused to collect and divert water on small shed, or as no-spill poultry feeders, fixed at a slight angle to a fence, with a small hole drilled in the bottom at one end to release any rainwater. This prevents waste of feed on the ground and discourages rodents too. Really, the list of innovations you can employ on your land is endless.

I was honoured to be chosen as winner of the Best Individual category at the Cornwall Sustainability Awards in 2014. As I progressed through the selection stages I was amazed that even the smallest changes we had incorporated in our day-to-day lives were highlighted as examples of best practice and innovation: to us they were just common sense. After the recognition I had been accorded, John and I continued to develop our aim to walk lightly on the earth, and to save money. As a sustainable, local producer I was happy to share my ideas with my customers, telling them about what I did and why I did it. They in turn felt good buying products that were produced ethically, and when they bought a bottle of cider, knew that it, literally, wasn't costing them the earth.

Soil

The soil on your smallholding or garden is the most important element of all, and hopefully, having read thus far in this book, you will agree. Without good, fertile soil the sustainable grower or producer will struggle, so let's have a look at what soil is, how it works and how we correct its composition.

Firstly, soil is made up of organic matter, rock particles of various sizes, water and air. Yup – that's it. There are three main types of soil, which you've heard TV gardeners talk about and see on the reverse of plant labels – heavy, light and medium. Heavy soil is made predominantly of clay particles – tiny little particles which clog together and don't allow water, air or nutrients to reach plants. Heavy soil can be recognised by having pools of water sitting on the surface after heavy rain, and supports reeds and acid loving plants. Light soil is dry and dusty. It's very free-draining as the particles are bigger and water drains though. But you can work both these types of soil to improve them. Heavy soil responds well to having lots of organic matter introduced. So, this means manure, compost and leaf mould. You can plough or dig it in, or even just spread on the surface and the earthworms will drag it down into the soil. Adding some larger particles such as gravel may be expensive, but this also will work in small areas. For dry soils, water retention will be the main issue and you can bulk up the soil again, by adding large quantities of organic matter. Hedging will also prevent wind erosion, and keep your light soil from blowing across the countryside. Now, medium soil is what most smallholders and gardeners want, and if you have this then fantastic – but you have to maintain it.

If you grow the same crops on the same piece of soil over many years you will eventually get problems. The soil will be depleted of certain nutrients and there also may be a build up of pests or diseases, which is why farmers and growers use crop rotation, and why traditional and organic farmers return organic matter to the soil. Buying in fertilizer will certainly replace the nutrients, but it doesn't add organic matter. There is nothing to feed the earthworms, insects and small creatures that help to keep our soil natural and productive.

Obviously, you can buy in loads of manure, spent mushroom

compost, old chicken litter from egg producers, but it's also really easy and cost effective to make your own, especially if you have a small or medium sized garden. Having a compost heap or a compost bin is easy to start and useful. They also reduce household waste if you compost all your green waste – fruit and vegetable peelings, old plastic free teabags, egg shells etc. You can add some newspaper, grass clippings, used animal bedding such as straw or hay and animal manure too. Autumn leaves can be composted together with kitchen and garden waste, or separately in chicken wire pens. Layering is the secret to success. Don't add huge amounts of grass clipping in one go – they will just sit there. Instead, try thin layers of fruit and vegetable peelings then a thin layer of grass clippings then something bulkier, such as old tomato plant stems or courgette stems and leaves, or straw. It will all start to break down and produce lovely organic compost. Adding chopped nettles will increase the fertility and having the male members of your family add urine to the heap will help it break down faster. Yes, although our urine is just as good as the guys, we ladies just aren't physically equipped to "deliver" this accelerator efficiently.

So, you've handled the composting side of feeding the soil, let's look at crop rotation. Now, the easiest way to explain this is to visualise three identical vegetable beds. If you grow potatoes and roots in the first one in the first year, then you'll need to plant them in the next bed (bed 2) the following year, and then into bed 3 the year after that. In year one, bed 2 could grow peas, beans onions and leeks, in year one bed 3 could grow cabbages, and other brassicas.

Three beds – move the vegetables along annually, a little like the Mad Hatter's tea party. This allows you to feed the hungry feeders once every third year, and prevents pest build up and nutrient deficiency.

Now, I've mentioned potatoes, brassicas and beans, but of

244

course you can grow whatever you like, and, if you have a small garden, I'd advise growing the things that cost more in the shops or markets. Why use that precious land to grow, if you'll excuse the pun, cheap-as-chips potatoes? I'd rather buy the potatoes from my local grower, and use my vegetable garden to grow things I value more – garlic, tomatoes, multi-coloured carrots, mixed salads, haricot vert. There is loads of info on no-dig systems at my friend Charles Dowding's website, **https://charlesdowding.co.uk/**.

I tend to plant my permanent fruit bushes, blackcurrants and gooseberries and the like, through mypex weed suppressing membrane. I site them along fences or to separate parts of the garden, and they need no real maintenance bar a little pruning over. I urge you to give growing your own a try. There really is nothing like fresh produce from your own soil.

Water & sewerage

Britain is immensely profligate with water: to drink, to wash in, to irrigate certain crops with, as a coolant in many industries, to flush away our bodily waste. But although water itself is free, collecting, purifying, and distributing it most certainly aren't, and reducing the use of mains water both in the home and on the farm is one of many strands in the pattern of making a smallholding pay. And quite apart from the dent water bills can make in your net profit, mains water isn't entirely sustainable. It's finite, and as the population grows the provision of adequate water and sewerage provision swallows up more and more investment. So, for the sake of your conscience and your wallet, plan to save water.

An obvious starting point is collecting rainwater from roof runoff. It can be used without filtration or chemical treatment for many purposes including irrigation and cleaning. And there's an awful lot of it. If we take an average monthly rainfall of 90mm and multiply it by the roof area we can harvest water from, we will get a volume. For example, a 10m x 4m building has a surface area of 40m² and so would harvest 3600L in an average month. Obviously therefore the potential exists to collect a large volume of water, and the standard domestic 200L water butt will be sadly inadequate.

If you're thinking of installing a serious rainwater harvesting system (RHS), look at Building Regulations Part G and H. BS8515 also contains guidance on the design, installation and maintenance of the supply of non-potable water systems. Different coloured pipe-work must be used to distinguish non-potable supplies from potable, and taps must be clearly labelled and have their handles removed to prevent accidental use. Systems are generally gravity-fed to above-ground circular butyl-lined tanks, stainless steel tanks, or lined reservoirs. Filtration systems are required to prevent blockages in pipes and pumping equipment.

The tank or tanks are going to be the most expensive part of the system, and they need to have an overflow capacity to allow for flushing out any debris. Ideally they should be integral to new builds but can be retrofitted. The Environment Agency suggests that costs can start at around £2,500. A quick trawl of the internet produces this complete system: **www.smithsofthedean.co.uk/rainsavers/rain-harvesting-system.html**. Maintenance is minimal and payback time will depend on the current cost of your water. For a cheaper DIY approach, you can buy suitable piping from any agricultural store or builders' merchant, while ordinary IBCs make durable and inexpensive holding tanks. Second-hand IBCs are easy to come by: for our cider production, I bought food-grade ones from Smith's, which also deals in used fruit juice/concentrate barrels and accessories. If the cost of installing a serious RHS looks alarming, just consider the possible savings. Charges for mains water range from £1 to £2 per cubic metre and are sure to rise in the future, and there's another charge if your waste water is discharged to a sewerage system. The average person uses 150 litres of water a day; smallholdings use a whole lot more, and even small changes round the house and buildings can make a difference. Using rainwater to flush the toilet could save 34 litres of water a day; that's 12.41m³ a year or £25 at £1.94 per cubic metre, and this is just for flushing the loo! Think of all the other on-farm applications you could supply from an RHS and count the savings.

An RHS will also reduce the volume of water entering your slurry stores, and washing foul water over your yards. This will help you to comply with Nitrate Vulnerable Zone regulations if you're in an area where nitrate pollution is a problem. More information on this is available from the Environment Agency. Untreated rainwater contains no chlorine and is therefore ideal for washing machinery, cleaning animal pens, irrigation, hydroponic systems, and crop-spraying. But it's not suitable for overhead irrigation on edible salads or fruit crops. Rainwater run-off will contain traces of environmental pollutants, animal and bird faecal matter, and vegetation such as moss, algae, and leaves. The roof itself can be a contaminant if it contains asbestos or lead. You may therefore still need filtration and/ or UV treatment for some crops and for animal and poultry drinking water. The Welfare of Farmed Animals (England) Regulation 2000 requires all animals either to have access to a suitable water supply and be provided with an adequate supply of fresh drinking water each day or be able to satisfy their fluid intake needs by other means. The National Dairy Farm Assurance Scheme (NDFAS) requires water for animal drinking to be fresh and clean. To put this in perspective, one dairy cow requires 60 litres of clean drinking water a day.

The Dairy Hygiene Regulations require water used to wash hands, udders and dairy machinery to be from a potable source. Normally this means mains water, but if you're not on the mains you have a couple of options. You can filter and treat your harvested rainwater so it's fit for consumption, but at a cost (although I would question the necessity of using rainwater for drinking anyway, unless you really are planning to live on an island or somewhere very, very remote). Even water from wells, streams and springs needs treatment: it's totally natural and may well contain iron, peat, nitrates, or even pathogens such as Cryptosporidium, E. coli and Campylobacter. Find out about water standards here **http://dwi.defra.gov.uk/consumers/advice-leaflets/standards.pdf**

A borehole is another option. This isn't simply a matter of drilling a well. The borehole will have to supply enough water of adequate quality for all your needs, which requires testing in advance. The British Geological Survey or the Geological Survey of Northern Ireland can prepare a prognosis for you for a fee, as indeed can many private companies. If both quality and quantity look likely to be sufficient, then you need consent from the Environment Agency or the Scottish Environment Protection Agency for a test hole. If that's all satisfactory you'll probably have to pay around £10,000 to get a working borehole drilled (to a minimum depth of 50m), lined, fitted with a motor pump and connected up, which will all take a few weeks. You may also need to register the borehole. Having said all that, you only need an abstraction licence (again, from the relevant Environment Agency) if you want to extract more than 20,000 litres a day; and once all the work is done and all the form-filling is out of the way you have a free source of water that will last for generations. However groundwater, whether from boreholes, wells or springs, also needs to be checked regularly for safety and you may still need sand filters and UV purifiers just as you would to render rainwater potable.

Producing less foul water, and making safe use of what you do produce, is another great saving, both environmentally and financially. You can, of course, stop flushing completely and use composting toilets instead. The simplest system is no more than a couple of buckets, one for liquids and one for solids, under a wooden stand with seats and lids fitted over them. Sprinkling sawdust from a handily placed bucket after use will stop them smelling (and if you still feel the need to use any cleaning products, make sure they're environmentally friendly – so, no bleach!). Keeping liquids and solids as separate as is feasible is important: type urine separator or diverter into your search engine and while away many a happy hour discovering and evaluating the various methods by which this may be achieved, **www.we-pee.com** is but one solution. The urine you collect can be used safely and effectively to activate a compost heap or diluted with five parts water as a soil conditioner: it's 95% water, with the rest made up of nitrogen-rich urea and minerals such as phosphorus and potassium, the very stuff that commercial fertilisers are made of and far too precious to waste.

The solids can be composted separately (not on the garden heap), for six months to a year in a septic tank or pit under a layer of soil or sawdust and then, like 77% of human sewage, spread over agricultural land or used as garden mulch. It's perfectly safe: according to Water UK, a trade body representing the water and sewerage corporations, "there are no reported cases of human, animal or crop contamination due to the use of sewage sludge on agricultural land". Common sense would however warn against using sewage from households where contraceptive pills, fertility treatments and HRT are being used, as the artificial hormones they contain contaminate the run-off from the soil and hence our waterways. (Manure from animals raised on growth hormones is equally harmful in this respect).

You can find construction plans for a simple compost toilet at **http://www.compostjunkie.com/composting-toilet-plans.html**; find more upmarket eco-toilets at **https://dunsterhouse.co.uk/eco-toilets-and-glamping-pods** (Common-or-garden septic tanks are still commonly used in the many rural areas that are still without mains sewerage, but have not been considered here because they don't in themselves save any water). Finally under this heading, grey water is the run-off from your bath, shower, hand-basin, kitchen sink, washing machine and other appliances whose waste water hasn't been in contact with human or animal faeces. It will contain traces of dirt, food, grease, hair, and household cleaning products but is nevertheless a safe and even beneficial source of irrigation water; but its nutrients become pollutants if allowed to run off into waterways. It can be used to water trees and gardens provided it doesn't come into direct contact with any fruit and vegetables that might be eaten raw. It should never be held in collection tanks for longer than 24 hours and shouldn't be allowed to puddle during use.

Heating & hot water including solar

More than half of all the money spent on fuel in Britain goes on keeping warm – that is, towards heating, cooking, and hot water. As I mentioned earlier in this section, we did not have the option of mains gas, and electricity for heating was too expensive, and so we installed a new woodburner with back-boiler. Installing a wood or multi-fuel stove is not something you can do yourself unless you have a HETAS qualification (visit **www.hetas.co.uk**). Incorrectly fitted appliances can release lethal carbon monoxide into a room. You'll also invalidate the warranty on the appliance and your insurer may well refuse to reimburse you for any loss or damage, and you will be unable to sell your property without the correct certification. You also need professional advice on the size, and how and where to site the appliance and radiators for maximum efficiency, which is a surprisingly technical subject.

What makes this kind of boiler of particular significance to the sustainable smallholder, though, is that once it's installed you can grow all the fuel you need, or find it locally to keep it going. Firewood has to be seasoned for at least a year to prevent tar building up in the flue, so we built two wood stores, one for fresh-cut wood and a second, nearer the house, for wood that was seasoned and ready to burn. We harvested coppiced willow as fuel and kindling from a shelter belt we'd planted. It actually proved useless as a windbreak; and we realised that hornbeam and beech were both much more effective in the hedge and also very good for fuel. There are many brands of appropriate stoves and cooking ranges available, some of which provide heating, hot water and cooking facilities. It's up to you to decide which is best for both your pocket and lifestyle.

Solar thermal – this is an evacuated (EV) solar tube panel supplied with a cylinder containing a coil as a heat exchanger. This is a different way of producing hot water, albeit not directly, and heating hot water (using a conventional electrical immersion in a hot water cylinder). This is an excellent option almost anywhere in the UK, as even the lowest light levels can generate hot water.

Electricity & lighting including solar

Solar Photovoltaic – If you are located from the midlands or further south and have a south-facing roof, you could install a solar PV system to generate electricity to offset the electricity costs of your home or home-based business. It will

251

depend on how the main house and other buildings are set up electrically and how the hot water is split as to what system would be most suitable, along with your electricity bills etc. Systems can be roof mounted or ground mounted, and you'll need to know whether you are on single or triphase electricity supply. The installation is simpler than an EV system, easier/cheaper for maintenance and more flexible than a combined EV/PV system.

A unit called an "Immersun" can be added into the system, which diverts any unused electricity to an existing electric hot water cylinder, adding to the heating ability of the system. This system is not as effective at producing hot water directly but the advantages are that when hot water is not needed the electricity will be used on other items within the home, reducing electrical consumption and therefore electrical bills.

We are considering a 6 panel system fitted with Immersun – quote for this in 2020 is around 8000€ (around £7300) just to give you an idea of prices. 3KW systems with 10 panels around 10,000 euros depending on mounting options and any add on batteries or Immersun – all set up and ready to go – approx 2-3 days install. A 6 panel system measures 3m x 3.3m or 10m^2 of roof space.

Generating electricity on a domestic scale is no big deal these days: every housing estate has a proportion of roofs (not a big enough proportion, though!) sporting those distinctive square black photovoltaic cells, and many benefit from the feed-in tariff, which closed in early 2019. But using solar PV to power your smallholding presents a dilemma you can only resolve for yourself. Solar power is DC; the grid is AC. The obvious thing to do, as with any domestic property, is smother all possible roofs, barns and outbuildings as well as the house itself, with PVs and subsidise your power consumption privately. The dramatic fall in installations since the FITs ended has resulted in a dramatic reduction in the cost of installation – £4-5,000 for an average house compared to £11,000 before.

If you can work from home and use the electricity you have generated to power both your house and the farmyard directly, having a professional installer discuss a suitable system for your needs can deal with the various technical difficulties arising from the need to switch current from DC to AC, which is what almost all domestic appliances run on. There are many companies supplying and installing domestic and larger systems, such as **www.navitron.org.uk**.

Solar panels are not the only way of generating your own power. Large wind turbines are responsible for providing more and more of the nation's electricity but scaled-down versions are generally only regarded as powerful enough for single-use appliances such as borehole pumps or on campsites. Integrated systems using solar with small wind turbines as back-up can prove highly effective, though. Vertical axis turbines, as at **www.leadingedgepower.com**, are much less obtrusive than the usual horizontally-mounted version with the propeller-type blades and are supposedly more efficient too.

There's a third option, too, more efficient than either sun or wind if sited correctly, and that's water. Provided there's a fast-running year round stream on your holding you can install one of any number of devices – Archimedes screw or paddle wheels for low-pressure flows on fairly flat land, submerged turbines for high-pressure mountain streams and larger rivers. Naturally, it's not as simple as it sounds: piping, small dams, millponds and other works might be necessary and will be pricey; you'll almost certainly need planning permission; and you still have the question of inverting DC to AC to resolve. For more on this and other issues related to sustainable energy visit **www.energysavingtrust.org.uk**.

Off-grid Living

Living entirely off the grid might be seen as a somewhat extreme version of sustainability, but a growing number of people are choosing complete self-sufficiency, as far it is possible; some out of conviction, some because it's the only way they can afford to live on their holdings, and some because their holdings are so remote there are simply no mains services or at least, getting connected would cost a fortune. You may have seen a few case studies featured on Ben Fogle's *New Lives in the Wild* TV series (new series on BBC TV in spring 2021).

Living off-grid is not an easy option. You have to be mentally, physically and financially fit to make a home, deal with your waste (*all* sorts of waste), source all your own utilities, and make a living while you're at it. And it's important not to allow yourself to become isolated: keeping at least some lines of communication open is not only vital to your mental wellbeing, but also of great practical value. "No man is an island", goes the saying, and one day you may find yourself requiring some sort of help, whether it be physical help or professional help.

If you have any doubts then start small, and perhaps go and stay in an existing off-grid community such as Tinker's Bubble in Somerset, or Brithdir Mawr in Powys for a while to see what it really entails. These communities are few and far between because of draconian planning restrictions and, let's be honest, a suspicious streak about alternative lifestyles among the local establishment.

Tinker's Bubble, a small woodland community in Somerset, was started in 1994 but has only ever had temporary planning permission. There are only a small number of permanent residents, but the community will accept new members and is a WWOOF host (Worldwide Organic Farmers &

Growers Volunteer Network). Run as an environmentally friendly enterprise, electricity is 12V, with spring water and composting toilets. Its income comes entirely from the land, including sales of firewood, charcoal, apple juice, jam, and woodland produce. There is a communal roundhouse and small sleeping units. The whole community shares chores and members work mainly outdoors. There are open days for you to come and see the set-up for yourself, and some short courses are available. For more details visit **www. tinkersbubble.org**.

The Centre for Alternative Technology in Maccynlleth, Powys, **www.cat.org.uk** is choc-full of innovative solutions in housing, energy generation, waste disposal and all other construction-related alternatives. A visit is enthralling and thought-provoking even if you're not particularly interested in the topic. It runs a number of courses for people who want to go off-grid.

The Centre for Sustainable Energy, **www.cse.org.uk**, offers practical help, guidance, and advice to sustainable energy projects from its base in Bristol.

Ben Law is probably the best known individual to live off grid, and lives and works at Prickly Nut Wood in West Sussex. He makes his living from coppicing and round-wood timber framing. He also runs courses and is a prolific author. Beginning many years ago by living on site in a yurt and caravan, he finally got permission to build his house, which was featured in Channel 4's Grand Designs programme and was the episode quickly became the viewing public's favourite build. The house is eco-friendly, with 12 volt electricity, hot water from a wood-fired range, solar shower and compost toilet. Ben has had an extensive relationship with his local planning department since he started to manage the woods over twenty years ago, and finally in 2012 obtained a change in the planning regulations regarding the ongoing permission for residential use for the house at Prickly Nut Wood (**www.ben-law.co.uk**).

Other must-visit sites are
www.thegreenlivingforum.net/forum
www.cropthornehouse.co.uk/design/
downsizer.net

Lifestyle Changes

There are just so many, but consider some of the following:

- Switch from disposable plastic lighters to matches.
- Cancel paper bank statements and go online.
- Grow your own produce and use a freezer.
- Use a pressure cooker to vastly reduce cooking time and fuel.
- Fix that dripping tap – 60 drips per minute equals 21 litres a day!
- If you have an open fire or woodburner, close the damper when not in use and prevent that hot air you've paid to heat from escaping up the chimney.
- Car share for work and to do the school run.
- Laundry – launder a full load, and reduce heat from hot to tepid wash. Dry on a line where possible. Try laundry detergent sheets to reduce plastic waste.
- Use passive solar gain in the house, even in winter. Installing outside shutters to windows keeps houses warmer in winter and cooler in summer.
- In the garden – remove sprinkers, water vegetables in early morning or late evening. Fill watering cans from waterbutts.

Agroforestry

Agroforestry, or forest gardening, can be described as the practice of having a land management system combining the growing of trees and shrubs within an arable or pasture environment. The practice of intercropping can help assist with increasing biodiversity, increasing soil fertility and easing of run-off problems. This is a traditional method of cultivation in areas of France and Italy and is becoming more attractive within sustainable farms in the UK. One such farm is Bluebell Farms in Cambridgeshire, where farmer Stephen Briggs has been experimenting with agro-forestry on his arable farm.

Originally a traditional fenland vegetable farm, Stephen switched to arable cropping and apple tree production. He advocates the agro-forestry system in his situation as it reduces the amount of soil erosion due to wind. On flat, open land (there are no hedges) loss of soil is a big issue. Instead of attempting to install windbreaks, Stephen has planted 85 culinary and dessert apple trees per hectare in alleys 24 metres wide with a spacing of 3 metres between each MM106 tree. This produces around 25 tonnes of fruit which is then either sold wholesale or juiced, whilst both utilising the space two metres above ground and creating a living, profitable windbreak. The roots of the apple trees go down a metre and therefore do not compete with the shallower rooting arable crops.

Of course, you can also intercrop with other fruit or nut trees or even soft fruit bushes, depending on your crops, location and climate. Stephen has produced a Nuffield Scholarship Report called *Agroforestry: A new approach to increasing farm production* in 2011 which can be found by searching the internet; another good starting point to research the subject is at the Agroforestry Research Trust **www.agroforestry.co.uk**

CASE STUDY –
Muxbeare Orchard

Dinah & Stig Mason
Muxbeare Orchard
Willand
Devon

The dream of a sustainable life on a smallholding turned into a four-year planning nightmare for Dinah and Stig Mason when they handed back the keys of their council flat in Hertfordshire and moved into a converted horsebox in a derelict four-acre orchard near Willand, Devon. It was 2009, and a £75,000 bequest from an aunt seemed to be the answer to the couple's prayers. Having kept a small amount of chickens, the dream was a fuller life on a self-sufficient and sustainable smallholding for their growing family.

The site seemed ideal. It had been neglected for 50 years, with the only building being a derelict barn, which the couple intended to renovate into a family home. Mid-Devon Council ruled that as the building was outside the existing village boundary, any development was prohibited as it constituted open farmland. There was also considerable opposition to development from neighbours and some villagers. Within a month the council served an enforcement notice requiring the family to leave the site. Meanwhile, the couple became involved in the community, charmed many locals and gained 1,400 signatures in support of their application to build a straw-bale house in the orchard. Permission was refused, and in June 2011 the council took them to county court where they were threatened with jail if they didn't comply. Naturally, they complied; for a time. In 2012 the Government released its new National Planning Policy Framework which substantially modified the previous rules governing residential development on agricultural land.

The clause that altered the Mason's case, clause 55, states: "Local planning authorities should avoid new isolated homes in the countryside unless there are special circumstances such as:

- the essential need for a rural worker to live permanently at or near their place of work in the countryside: or
- where such development would represent the optimal viable use of a heritage asset or would be appropriate enabling development to secure the future of heritage assets; or
- where the development would re-use redundant or disused buildings and lead to an enhancement to the immediate setting; or
- The exceptional quality or innovative nature of the design of the dwelling."

This sudden change obliged the council to allow the Masons to bring their horsebox back to the orchard. The council refused permission for the straw-bale house, but in 2013 approved the more expensive restoration and conversion of the barn. The family moved in to their almost completely off-grid home in 2015, where they run and make their living from what is almost the ideal sustainable smallholding. With solar power, a woodburning stove and rainwater harvesting, they keep pigs, chickens and geese. Vegetables are grown in field and polytunnel, and the orchard supplies apples for eating, cooking, juice and cider. They drew the attention of Ben Fogle, who featured the family in his Channel 5 series, *New Lives in the Wild UK (2015)*, and who has recently returned to make a follow-up programme, which will be aired in early 2021.

Dinah has set the family's goals and achievements simply:

- To live sustainably to feed ourselves and our family
- To give back to the local and surrounding communities
- To give our children the knowledge of living within the seasons, growing local organic food.
- To look-after our children as full-time parents and part-time workers.
- To live in a low-impact traditionally built house constructed from natural materials on a smallholding, working with the orchard and growing organic food.

*****

Lorraine Turnbull has written many books including:

The Sustainable Smallholders' Handbook (2019)

How to Live the Good Life in France (2020)

Living off the Land: My Cornish Smallholding Dream (2020)

You can also visit Lorraine's Facebook page @Sustainable Smallholding for loads of information and photographs.

Appendix –
More information

How to Humanely kill a Chicken

I've tried the 'wring the neck at arms length' method, but can't physically do it. As a woman my arms simply aren't long enough. So, I have learned the "broomstick" method. It's foolproof, and once learned will deliver a quick, clean death. It's also a good method for those who are squeamish as it offers a degree of separation between the human and the bird.

First of all, don't use a broomstick – it's far too large in diameter to do the job cleanly. Find or buy metre-long length of 12 or 13 mm round steel bar. This will be your broomstick.

Remove the bird from the others (easier when they are in their house), holding it securely and taking it to a quiet area. Place the bird facing down on the ground, whilst keeping tight hold of the legs. Place the metal bar over the back of the neck. You will know you have the right place as the bar will neatly sit in the little hollow where the neck and the skull meet. So you now have a "cross" made of the bar lying at right angles to the head and body of the bird.

Use both hands to firmly grip the legs as far up the bird as you can comfortably.

Place one foot firmly on the bar about a foot away from the head. Repeat with the other foot on the other side. Pull sharply and firmly up and forward in a smooth but forceful pull. You should feel the neck go instantly, but if it's your first time you'll be nervous and may not notice. How hard to pull is the question I'm always asked. This is hard to answer as we all have different ideas of what "sharply and firmly" is.

Practice will perfect your method, but if you are pulling the bird's head off then you are pulling too firmly. The head dislocates from the neck, pulling the spinal cord out of the base of the skull and rendering death very quickly and painlessly.

The bird will start to flap (keep a good hold of the legs), which may take a few minutes to subside (less if the bird was near death). This is muscle reaction only. The bird has been dead since you pulled the bird up and forward, with the bar over its neck.

Prepare A Chicken For The Oven

Having bred poultry for quite some time, I always had a surplus of cockerels, which naturally were eaten. Actually, our own poultry became so popular with the family that instead of just doing the odd one for a roast, I now use the meat for chicken fajitas, kebabs, casseroles, in pasta dishes and of course soup.

Of course you have to start with a bird. You'll get more meat on a large fowl, dual purpose or meat bird. I have bred and eaten both Light Sussex and Maran (both dual purpose breeds), and have to say that the Maran was marginally more popular with the family, with quite a lot of breast meat, and a slightly superior taste. Birds bred exclusively for meat include the Cobb or Ross commercial meat strains.

263

I have eaten a bird at 16 months old, and wouldn't repeat the experience. Although the breast meat was tender enough, the legs were very tough, and after much experimenting, we fattened our birds to be ready at about 4-6 months old.

The afternoon before they are due to be killed we withhold food, but allow them water. Early the next morning, they are taken from their house and killed immediately to avoid distress. We find that in the winter, when the mornings are dark, they are usually a little sleepy and it's all done before the bird has properly woken up, with very little stress at all. Neck dislocation is our favoured method – it's quick and absolute. Once the bird has been killed there are two ways that you can prepare the meat for cooking.

Jointing

This is the quickest and easiest method – so perfect for beginners. Please note that using this method removes the skin from the bird: you are left with bare fillets and joints. If you don't feel confident with eviscerating (gutting) a bird, then I suggest this method.

Place your dead bird on a clean, dry work surface and part the feathers with your hands just under where the wing joins the body; what we would call the armpit. Insert a sharp knife here to open the skin, and then tear or cut to reveal the flesh underneath. You need to be aiming to pull the skin away from the flesh on the breast of the bird, almost like removing a glove. You should now have the whole breast area revealed, which you simply remove from the bird with a sharp knife. Run the knife along the breastbone slowly, slipping the knife gently under the breast fillet, parting it from the underlying ribcage. Place the fillet on a clean, dry plate and turn bird over, repeating as for the other side. To get the drumsticks, firstly again part the feathers, slit the skin open and pull away to reveal the area on which you will be working on. I force the leg to disjoint at what we would call the hip. Use a sharp knife to cut away the flesh where it joins the body. This is quite fiddly, so take your time. When you have removed the legs from the body, you will probably want to remove the feet. This is easily done with a sharp axe on a wooden block. Finally, rinse all your joints and fillets in cold running water, before either freezing or preparing to cook.

Preparation For Roasting

The second method is a little trickier. Firstly you will have to pluck your bird. This is best performed whilst the bird is still warm, as it allows easier removal of feathers. I hang the birds at eye level on baler twine in a draught-proof shed (less feathers blowing around). Gently strip a small amount of feathers from the body at a time, working over the whole carcass, except the head and neck. You can wet pluck a bird, but a dry plucked bird keeps for longer.

Take your plucked bird to a clean dry worktop or table. A strategically placed bucket (with a bag or plastic sack inside) will allow you quick disposal of all waste, and another bucket with warm water will allow you to rinse your hands if you should need.

With a sharp knife cut through the neck skin close to the body all around the neck, revealing the neck which you cut through with a pair of boning scissors or sharp secateurs and remove. Gently insert fingers into the neck opening and feel downwards for the crop (You may feel remnants of grain in this). Ease the crop out without breaking it and discard. At this point it's a good idea to remove the legs at the knee joint. You can either use boning scissors or a clean, sharp knife to do this.

Next, place the bird on its back with its legs facing you and cut a small circle with a sharp knife around the vent of the bird, taking care not to puncture the intestine. Ease this out in one piece if you can, and enlarge the slit slightly to allow you to get your hand inside the bird. Remove everything from inside the bird. Most of the insides should all come away together, leaving the lungs adhering to the walls of the cavity. These can be removed by sliding your open hand inside the cavity easing matter away from the sides.

If you push your hand further up you should feel the end of the windpipe, which you can pull on to remove. Sometimes it is very slippery, and a clean tea towel or kitchen towel may help you get a better grip. The bits you have removed from the bird include the offal, which I personally discard. However, you can use the neck for soup stock and many people eat the heart and liver. All that remains is for you to rinse out your bird with cold running water and disposal of the waste materials. To finish I simply tie the bird's legs together with a small piece of string and then it's ready for roasting.

Main points to remember

- keep work surfaces clean
- rinse fillets or carcase in clean cold running water
- place meat for eating on a clean plate
- refrigerate or freeze as soon as possible
- cook thoroughly

How to Make Cider for your own use.

The Fruit

Cider can be made from almost any type of apple. However, you will get a more complex flavour if you use a mix of apple types – dessert, cookers and cider apples. Think of dividing apples into four tastes – sweets, sharps, bittersweets and bittersharps. The last two are found in cider apples because of the high concentration of tannin. If you don't have access to cider apples, try adding some crab apples to supply the tannins.

Apples are ripe when the pips are brown, the skin "gives" slightly when pressed with a thumb and the skin has a waxy appearance (obviously not for russets). You can ripen apples by storing for a few days. Don't use mouldy fruit for cider. (For juicing, apples must be free from any cuts/damage/mould and picked from the tree.) Basically if you wouldn't take a bite out of it – compost it.

Sunshine turns the starch in apples to sugar, so a good summer will produce sweeter apples. It is the sugar that turns to alcohol. After you press the juice, you can test the "specific gravity" (SG), using a hydrometer (ca £5). A reading of 1.070 should result in a finished cider of around 8.5 %; SG 1.045 and a potential alcohol of 6%. If the juice SG is less than 1.045 and you have no sweeter juice for blending, it should be brought up to this level by the addition of sugar, or the resultant alcohol level may not be sufficient to protect the final cider during storage. To raise the SG in 5° steps, dissolve 12 - 15 grams of sugar in each litre of juice and re-test with the hydrometer until the desired level is reached.

Milling and Pressing

If you want to make more than 100 litres, I'd suggest hiring a Speidel mill or fruit shark. Small quantities of apples can be processed with a food processor in the kitchen. Whatever you use, thorough cleaning afterwards is essential to prevent the acid eating into the metal blades. The resulting pulp will soon discolour. When making juice (**not cider**) you can add Ascorbic acid (5g per 10L of juice) powder whilst pulping and mix it in to prevent juice going brown. We use a rack and cloth press and the juice is collected in food-safe containers and transferred to fermentation vessels. The amount of juice depends on the variety of apples. Russets for example always give less juice than desert apples, but you can expect 25kg producing around 16-18 litres of juice.

Fermentation and storage

We try to make cider traditionally, and don't add sugar to increase the alcohol level, but we don't just let the juice sit with no help. So initially, we let the juice sit overnight and this allows a small amount of wild yeast to begin working. At the start of this stage I take both a pH reading to establish how acid the juice is, and an initial SG reading to check how much sugar is in the juice, using the hydrometer. I record all this on a batch sheet. The next day we add sodium metabisulpite. The formula we use is 10g to 100ml of water to make a 5% solution. Then 1ml of this per litre of juice. Mix in well.

Acidity and pH

The acidity is controlled more by the variety of fruit than the climate. As beginners we are just looking at pH. Narrow range pH indicator sticks or papers (e.g. pH 2.8 to 4.2) are now available cheaply from some home brewing suppliers. A desirable juice pH range for cider-making is from 3.2 - 3.8. Many traditional bittersweet cider apples tend to be high in pH which is why they need blending with more acid fruit, preferably before fermentation. That is one reason why bittersharp apples, such as "Kingston Black", are highly regarded in terms of their composition for single-variety cider making. If juice is too acidic you can raise the pH by adding a little calcium carbonate to neutralise it, in 1 gram per litre steps.

You can add sugar or water etc at this stage, but excessive dilution (over 15%) will make the cider "thinner" in its overall complexity of flavour. The juice should now be housed in a suitable clean vessel for fermentation. You must also have some sort of "airlock", fitted shortly after fermentation starts, to allow carbon dioxide gas to escape but to prevent air getting in.

The next addition is that of yeast nutrient, which is sometimes needed by the yeast for its own growth. Your fermentation rate will probably be much improved if you add these. The fermentation is also less likely to "stick", or to grind to a halt before completion. The cider can therefore be racked and bottled sooner, reducing the chances of spoilage in store.

Sodium metabisulphite

Next, you add the Sodium metabisulphite (Campden tablets), which inhibit growth of spoilage yeasts and bacteria, while allowing "good" yeasts to dominate. The table below shows the appropriate levels to use. As you gain experience and confidence you can choose to reduce or omit it.

Addition of Sodium metabisulphite

Juice pH	SO2 needed in parts per million (ppm)	Campden Tablets per gallon or ml. of 5% SO2 stock solution per litre
Above 3.8 (insipid)	.....Lower pH to 3.8 with addition of malic acid.....	
3.8 - 3.5	150	3
3.5 - 3.3 (balanced)	100	2
3.3 - 3.0	50	1
Below 3.0 (sharp)	None	None

The Yeast

Choose a white wine or cider yeast, and follow the directions. If sulphur dioxide is used, it is also important to wait overnight before adding the yeast culture. Fermentation should commence within 48 hours if an active yeast culture is used. Wild yeasts will take longer and will begin to die after a few days as the alcohol level rises, leaving the fermentation at the mercy of any other dominant organism which has been able to establish itself.

You can skip the nutrients unless the fermentation begins to "stick". The progress of the fermentation should be monitored weekly with a hydrometer and the fall in SG plotted on a graph against time (a fall of one degree SG per day is pretty reasonable). This makes it much easier to see whether sticking is occurring, and the nutrient and vitamin can be added then if necessary.

Conduct of the fermentation

Initially, there is considerable frothing and production of carbon dioxide. A loose plug and the outpouring of gas will probably ensure that nothing undesirable can creep back into the fermentation vessel. When the initial frothing subsides, top up with juice and fit an airlock to ensure that the flow of gas remains one-way. As fermentation progresses, it will begin to level off and you should consider the first racking of the cider from its yeast at an SG of 1.005. If it stops fermenting at an SG much higher than this, then it may be "stuck", and nutrient addition together with a good stir may help the yeast to grow again. It may also stop if the temperature falls too low, but when the weather warms up again, the fermentation should re-commence.

The first racking should be into another clean vessel, trying to leave behind as much lees as possible and with the minimum of aeration to the cider. Best done on a cold day, use a clean plastic syphon tube fixed to a plastic rod so it rests just above the yeast deposit or, on a larger scale, with a suitable pump. The transferred cider should be run gently into the bottom of the new vessel without splashing. It is important to minimise the headspace and to **prevent air contact as much as possible.** This is why some people add 50 ppm of sulphur dioxide at every racking, although at the first racking this is probably unnecessary because of the remaining carbon dioxide.

Maturation and Bottling

After the first racking the air-lock is re-fitted, and examined for further gas evolution, and then topped up with water or cider and tightly closed. The cider may remain in this state for several weeks, before a final racking to a closed container for bulk storage or directly into bottle. Don't let it sit on the lees for more than 2 weeks. Occasionally if the ferment goes on into the spring, you may get a malo-lactic or secondary fermentation.

A finished cider will benefit from maturing for at least 2 months (we do three months), as the flavour stabilises, and the harsher notes are smoothed out. A dry cider with no added sugar and sufficient alcohol should be quite stable in clean, closed and well-filled bottles, and should stand a minimal risk of any unwanted conversion to vinegar! Personally, I would borrow or hire a pasteuriser, and pasteurise glass bottles at 68 degrees for 20 minutes, then remove from pasteuriser, rest on their side on towels to pasteurise inside the cap or lid. The process kills all bacteria and yeast, and if done correctly, will allow for storage for up to two years.

Flow Chart for Cidermaking

MAIN PROCESS	OPTIONS
Apples	Selection of variety
Harvest	
Storage	Fruit blending?
Washing	
Milling/pulping	
Pressing	pH adjustment? SO_2 addition, yeast addition?
Fermentation	Adding nutrient? Adding sugar?
Racking	SO_2 addition?
Storage/maturation	Adding sweetener? Pasteurisation?

How To Graft Apple Trees

There are two main techniques for grafting fruit trees – whip grafting, where a short piece of scion wood is attached to the rootstock in early spring, producing a single stem one-year old tree by the following summer, and bud grafting, where a single bud is attached to an actively growing rootstock in the summer time. Whip grafting allows the tree to develop more quickly because it uses a larger piece of the scion wood, and is marginally easier for beginners; however, bud grafting produces a straighter tree and a stronger union, and can be done as a back-up plan to failed whip grafts.

Selecting Scion Wood

Choose a healthy tree and if possible, use well ripened, mature green wood from the outside/sunny side of the tree.

Cut a 7.5-10cm whip with three buds present:

1. Stock bud: just behind the grafting cut, helps with callusing

2. Top bud: to form the shoot

3. Middle bud: back-up if the top bud fails

Attaching the Scion to the Rootstock

Cut back the rootstock to between 15-30cm – too low a graft union invites pathogen risk from splash back from the soil. Too high, especially on dwarfing rootstock, can make for a weak union. This can be done on bare root rootstocks on a table, or in-situ on a tree growing in the ground.

The ends of each joining piece should be cut in matching clean elliptical slices so that when joined together, as much of the cambium layer (the green part of the wood between the outer bark and the woody bit) as possible is touching. You must also avoid your fingers touching the cambium

273

layer, as this will render the graft useless. This may take some practice! Leave a small "church window" of internal scion wood sticking over the top of the rootstock wood to help with callusing. Bind tightly, and securely with grafting tape. A few dots of horticultural wax to seal the cut open areas could also be employed and will prevent water loss. If conducted in early February, you should see new green growth from the scion by May. If the scion looks dry or indeed detaches from the rootstock it's a fail and you could try again with bud grafting in late June or July.

For bud grafting, look for a plump, healthy looking bud from the outside/sunny side of the tree that is not dry and shrivelled or with obvious damage to create your scion. Using a grafting knife, cut a small horizontal slit into the bark ½ an inch underneath the bud and slowly pull the knife upwards taking in the cambium layer and outer bark without cutting into the heartwood, or inner part of the branch. End the slice ½ an inch above the bud, so it comes away neatly.

Cut a 1 inch vertical slit into the rootstock where the bud will be placed, cutting only into the bark layer. At the top of this incision, cut a cross-wise slit, creating a T-shape. Then, gently lifting the corners where they meet (with a knife), slide in the scion bud with the growing tip pointing upwards, ensuring that the cambium layers on each are touching. Again, avoid touching either of the prepared surfaces with your fingers. Wrap the join tightly in grafting tape to keep dry and in the following spring prune off the tip of the branch as soon as the grafted bud begins to grow.

Woodburners & Multifuel Burners

One of the issues that smallholders are faced with is how to efficiently heat your home, faced with the ever increasing prices and availability of fossil fuels. With running costs expected to increase by at least 40%, or more if you live in a rural property, we should all look at how efficient our heating is. This has in turn led to an increased interest in alternative renewable fuels.

Here, I explain the different types of domestic appliances on the market, which will help you to decide which is the best for your circumstances. There is also a handy checklist of annual maintenance that smallholders can easily do themselves.

Range Of Appliances

There are a range of typical wood and multi-fuel burners on the market. Firstly, the open fire, which was the most common form of heating in the average home in the UK until the 1940s. Woodburners and multifuel burners had a surge of popularity in the 1950s and 60s, when self-sufficiency first became popular. Today, there are a multitude of makes and styles, from traditional to contemporary. More recently, cutting edge technology has introduced wood pellet boilers and stoves to the market.

Many of us older folks can remember sitting in the front room or parlour, in front of an open fire. The chairs were scorched on the side nearest the fire, and the back of the room usually cold. And granny hated it when the smuts from the fire got all over the clothes drying in front of the fire!

The advantages of wood or multifuel burners over the open fire are many. There is more heat conveyed to the room, and less going up the chimney, the fire is contained safely behind glass, and the woodburner does not require emptying daily. The disadvantages are that if you wish to keep the stove going all night, you really need to add coke briquettes or large logs to the last top-up, and damp it down with some powdery coke.

Wood pellet boilers and room heaters use waste wood products, can be automatically fed, and are highly efficient, with very little wasted heat. They can be expensive to buy and install, are a little noisier, and more suitable for constant heating.

- Open fires – 15-20% efficient
- Wood/multifuel burners – 70-80% efficient
- Wood pellet heaters/boilers – 90% efficient

Stove Output

Heat output is measured in kilowatts (kW). When working out the kW output required for your room, remember that variables such as poor insulation, large windows or patio doors will require a greater output. To calculate the heat requirement for your room multiply the heightXwidthXdepth of the room in metres and divide by 12. Now you know the size and output of appliance, say 4.5kW or 6kW, that you'll require.

Cast Or Steel?

- Cast stoves take longer to heat up and retain heat longer
- Cast stoves have a darker look, and can be very ornate.
- Steel stoves have a lighter, bluish tone.
- Both types have to be used in accordance with the manufacturer's instructions. If misused, cast stoves can crack, and steel stoves can warp.

276

Location Of The Stove

If you have a two-storey house, then the best location for a room heating stove would be centrally located in the hall, to allow heat to naturally rise and heat more of the building space. However, it is more usual to find a stove located in a specific room, say the living room or kitchen. If there is a fireplace, then the stove can stand in front of it, or if it is a recessed or inglenook, then the stove can be sited within it. The drawback here is that heat is lost to the walls.

Chimneys

- You don't need a chimney to have a solid fuel burning appliance
- You will need Building Regulations approval to install a woodburner if you do not use a HETAS installer.
- You can only burn wood in a smoke control area in an exempt appliance

Many people think that because they don't have a chimney, they can't have a wood or multifuel burner. Nowadays, installers regularly fit twin-wall insulated flues, which safely convey heat and smoke away from the appliance. If you do have a chimney, have it inspected prior to buying your appliance. A simple smoke test can determine the health (or otherwise) of your chimney fabric. Nowadays, fitters almost always insist on the fitting of a chimney liner. Chimneys function better with some sort of cowl to prevent water entering and cooling the chimney. Two angled slates are sufficient, if cemented into place.

Main Controls In A Wood Or Multifuel Burner

The **glass door** is kept tightly shut except when lighting, restocking or cleaning out. Correct burning will keep the glass clean.

The **damper** is usually fitted in the outlet to the flue pipe and controls the draw in the chimney. You'll use this control more when you burn wood alone.

The **coal grate** comes with multifuel stoves, but can be removed if you burn wood only. Keep it in place if you burn a mixture of wood and coal or smokeless fuel.

The **riddle** is sometimes combined with the grate, and allows fine ash and waste to fall into the ash tray below, and allows air circulation in burning material.

The **bottom ventilator,** which can be a dial or sliding system underneath the glass door, or can be combined with the door for the ash tray, is used to control the air entering beneath the grate. This is usually closed when you burn wood only.

Some appliances have **air wash vents** (usually a dial or slide vent above the door). This is used to "wash" the glass with air and is designed to keep the glass clean during burning.

The **ash tray** needs emptying when full. Ash from burnt wood can be returned to the garden.

Finally, as we head for a tightening of our purse-strings, sit down and do your sums. If you have a source of timber available to you, then there really is nothing as cheering to come home to as a real fire.

Welding For Smallholders

With the right equipment and knowledge any smallholder, male or female, can effectively and competently weld and repair items such as tractors, trailers, gates, and other metal objects. Late autumn through to spring is the ideal time to service and repair the many farm implements and machinery that have developed damage or faults. This is such a handy skill to learn that I urge you to attend a class locally to learn how to use one safely and competently.

Firstly, there are a few different types of welding and welder, but for the average smallholder, an Inverter ARC welder is perfect for most needs.

What items can be repaired by welding?

Well, obviously they need to be metal! In fact any items fabricated in mild steel are suitable for welding. This includes link boxes, trailer sides, gates and hurdles, animal pens, tractors, and many farm implements. If you need to weld something out in the fields where you don't have an electricity supply you will need a gas welding set or a mobile generator, or you could power an inverter from a generator. If you felt you could have a great deal of remote jobs to do, you could invest in a mobile welder (petrol or diesel powered).

** ITEMS NOT TO WELD **

Do not weld structural parts, lifting equipment, towing hitches, tractor safety frames, pressure vessels, fuel tanks etc. An expert welder is required for these jobs, and in the event of failure you may find yourself on the wrong side of the law or even cited in a compensation claim!

If you decide to weld a motor vehicle or tractor, disconnect the battery earth first and unplug the alternator or you could end up with damage to the alternator.

What do I need to get started?

Firstly, for safety, you require steel toe-cap boots or shoes, thick gauntlets, a decent boiler suit, safety glasses and a welding mask. If you are serious about welding, you can buy a mask with an auto-darkening visor, which will cost about £60. The equipment is necessary, as unprotected skin can be burnt easily whilst welding, and a very uncomfortable night with 'ARC-eye' can be spent if you have the misfortune to have had your unprotected eyes flashed whilst welding. Pliers or tongs are handy for handling hot metal, and a chipping hammer to assist in slag removal.

Welding set equipment

A brand new ARC welder (240 volt single phase) could cost you between £100 and £200, but you could purchase a second-hand one from £50 upwards. A set with an output of 180 amps is ideal for most farm workshop repairs and fabrication. An inverter can come with a 240 volt supply or with 110 volt supply, and is basically a very portable lightweight welder capable of welding up to130 amps (so for small jobs) and would cost around £300 new.

To further complicate matters welders are also available as air-cooled or oil-cooled. You basically get what you pay for, so do your homework. All welding equipment should have a regular service and safety check, paying particular attention to any damaged cables. Always have the main isolator switch within easy reach. You will also need to buy welding rods (electrodes), which come in various thicknesses, but for most welding 2.5 mm & 3.2 mm max will suffice.

How to install and set up the welding set

The process

After dressing in your safety gear, and wearing your safety glasses (you only get one pair of eyes), you need to clean down the item requiring welding with a grinder or file. Decide if it requires a simple weld (a join), or the insertion of a plate of metal, or in the worst case, a complete cut out of the corroded material and replacement of the component part.

If, for example, a simple join or butt weld is required, set the two plates together leaving an appropriate gap (one third the thickness of the material), tack weld together (see below), de-slag (see below) and wire brush. Hold the electrode holder at an angle of around 60-70 degrees and if you are right handed, weld from left to right. Then weld together with a single run and no weaving. De-slag and wire brush. Check back of weld for penetration. If possible weld this side also.

How to Tack weld

This is basically using a few "spots" of welding to hold the pieces in position until welded completely. Tacking allows you to reposition if necessary.

How to De-slag

This is basically chipping the slag (or residue) off of the weld with a chipping hammer. Slag looks like a black crust. Best chipped off when the weld is cooling. Finish with a wire brush before welding again.

Signs of a good weld

- correct width of bead
- an arc with a good steady crackling sound
- the correct amount of reinforcement
- no undercut
- good penetration
- a smooth, even appearance indicating the correct rod angle.

Summary

- **Try to get someone experienced to teach you**
- **Always wear safety gear**
- **Start with simple items**
- **Use the correct electrode to the material to be welded**
- **Weld in a single smooth run**
- **Try to keep your feet dry or you may become the earth!**

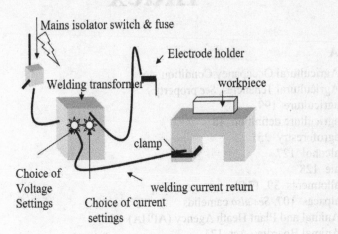

Mains isolator switch & fuse

Electrode holder

workpiece

Welding transformer

clamp

Choice of Voltage Settings

Choice of current settings

welding current return

Index